Cooking for a crowd

Cooking for a crowd

Christa Welgemoed

Human & Rousseau
Cape Town • Johannesburg • Pretoria

Dedicated to my husband, Tinus

Acknowledgements
I would like to thank the following bodies and institutions:
The Meat Board on behalf of the Red Meat
Industry of South Africa
The Department of Food and Textile Technology,
Pretoria Technicon
Red Wing Poultry Farm
Early Bird Farm (Pty) Ltd (Goldi)
Concordia Poultry and Rabbit Abattoir

First edition 1995
Second edition 2000

Published by Human & Rousseau (Pty) Ltd
Design Centre, 179 Loop Street, Cape Town
English translation by Pat Barton
Illustrations by Louwra Marais
Photography by Willie van Heerden
Styling by Christa Welgemoed and Myrna Klerck
Dishes prepared by Christa Welgemoed and Myrna Klerck
Pottery supplied by Elza Pragt (photo, p. 34-35) and Esias Bosch (photo, p. 13)
Typography and cover design by Etienne van Duyker, ALINEA STUDIO, Cape Town
Typeset in 10 on 11 pt Garamond ITC, Cape Town
Printed and bound by Colorcraft, Hong Kong

ISBN 0 7981 4118 2

CONTENTS

An asterisk (*) after the name of a recipe in a menu indicates that it appears on the same page or elsewhere in the book. Please consult the index for the relevant page number, if necessary.

Important
All the ingredients listed below the menu are uncooked, unless otherwise stated.

FOREWORD

It's now widely accepted that hospitality and the pleasure of eating well are synonymous; there are also numerous sources that can be consulted when you are entertaining a small group of people. The problem arises, however, when the group consists of 12 or more people, and you are entertaining at home.

This book is intended to be a guide when you have 12, 24 or 48 guests to entertain. To make planning easier, a full menu has been provided with each main course. Where necessary, recipes for first courses, side dishes and desserts are provided, and information on portion sizes and quantities needed is given throughout.

There are five sections – divided according to budget restrictions and the occasion – offering dishes to suit every pocket and taste. All the recipes have been standardised for domestic equipment, so that they can be prepared easily in the home kitchen.

Pocket-wise menus provides a number of recipes and menus specially put together for the economy-minded hostess, using everyday, readily available ingredients. These dishes are also perfect for church and school functions, and for camps.

For those who enjoy entertaining a large group of friends without too much effort, *Food for friends* is ideal. It offers a wide and interesting choice, ranging from one-dish meals to delicious food cooked over the coals.

Hassle-free get-togethers contains simple dishes that require little last-minute preparation. And when you're planning a buffet, the recipes in *Sit-down dinners* are just the thing. Although these are more formal dishes, very few of the more expensive meat cuts are called for.

Finally, there's a section that provides for extra-special occasions. In *Nothing but the best*, I have brought together an exciting selection of menus and dishes – perfect for that very smart dinner that everyone will talk about for ages!

The ideas, menus and recipes were chosen in such a way that they can be swopped around according to your taste. It requires very little effort to mix and match them, until you have the menu that suits your specific circumstances.

Good luck and happy home entertaining!

Christa Welgemoed

Important
The recipes in this book were tested in specific cookware not necessarily available to all. Only A grade meat was used; B and C grade meat could, therefore, take longer to become tender.

INTRODUCTION

Planning is essential

When a large group of people are to be entertained – at home or in a hired venue – thorough planning is absolutely essential. By working systematically, potential problems are eliminated and the work load is spread evenly. Planning also makes budget control and preparation easier and prevents unnecessary waste. The following aspects are important in the planning of a function:

The occasion

☐ What is the occasion?
☐ Who are the guests?
☐ When is the function?
☐ Where will it be held?

These four questions, along with budget considerations, are the departure point for planning a function.

The menu

After you've decided when and where to hold the function, how many people you are going to invite and so on, it's time to plan the menu. Remember the following:

Above left: Fresh green salad (menu, p. 84). Above right: Aniseed carrots (p. 91). Bottom right: Oven-roasted pepper Scotch fillet (p. 84) with Mock pesto sauce (p. 84). Bottom left: Kassler rib with apricot glaze (p. 81).

☐ Make your planning departure point the main course; the kind of meat, for example, and the cooking method. Always bear in mind the cooking facilities at your disposal. These include kitchen space oven space, chilling facilities and help with serving.
☐ Choose the accompaniments to complement this main course, for example:

– Meat dish (three-layer fillet)
– Starch dish (roast potatoes)
– Vegetable 1 (carrots with orange)
– Vegetable 2 (French green beans)
– Salad (mixed salad with feta cheese)

Take into account the colours of items on the menu. The shape of the items also differs greatly; for example, round potatoes and long green beans. The vegetable dishes are comparatively simple, as the meat dish is more complex and requires a good deal of preparation time. Complete the menu by adding the first course and the dessert. (See the box at the top of p. 10.)

☐ After the dishes have been chosen, you can go on to make a list of alcoholic and other beverages. The occasion, the guests and the budget are all factors that affect your choice. (See *Drinks* for more information and general tips.)

Calculating costs

Calculate the cost of the menu and check it against the planned budget. If it exceeds the budget, you can adapt the menu according-

Salmon with sour cream dill sauce
Whole-wheat bread

Three-layer fillet
Roast potatoes
Carrots with orange
French green beans
Mixed salad with feta cheese

Fresh strawberries and home-made ice cream

ly. In the example given, for instance, you could use a cheaper fish than salmon. It's better to use cheaper starters and desserts than to change the focus of the menu, the main course.

Purchases
Draw up detailed lists of purchases, showing item, description and quantity. Divide the lists according to place of purchase (for example, vegetables and fruit, meat, dairy products, groceries and drink) so that the shopping expedition takes as little time as possible.

You could also draw up lists for items that can be purchased a week in advance (non-perishables), two days before (vegetables and fruit, if you have sufficient cooling facilities) and on the day of the function (highly perishable items like fresh cream).

Remember to order scarce or hard-to-find items well in advance and, afterwards, to confirm that they will, indeed, be available. Always have an alternative in mind if the products are not available.

Work schedule
A carefully planned work schedule is indispensable. Having one avoids unnecessary piling up of jobs and ensures that everything goes as smoothly as possible.

Ask a friend or your daughter, if she's handy about the house, to help you during the busiest times. See the sample schedule on p. 11 for the day before as well as the day of the function:

Tips for purchasing

☐ Buy good-quality products to prevent waste.

☐ Plan your shopping trip in such a way that the perishables are bought last and so do not have to be in a hot car for too long, thereby risking any chance of spoilage.

☐ Take a coolbox with you when buying frozen products, to ensure optimal quality.

☐ Always buy a little more than is called for. There could be wastage; for instance, fruit and vegetables could have bad spots that were not visible at first.

Meat could shrink more than anticipated as a result of using a larger cooking surface, or of having to cook the meat longer than recommended in the standardised recipe.

(It is important to remember that these recipes were tested in specific cookware not necessarily available to all, and that only A grade meat was used. B and C grade meat could, therefore, take a little longer to become tender.)

☐ If the menu specifies items that are not in season, save by replacing these items with something similar, but cheaper.

☐ Buy meat or fish from a dealer you know well. Asking him to help you select the kind of meat, to bone and tie the meat, or to cut the meat into the desired portion sizes, all saves valuable time.

☐ To avoid disappointment, note the expiry dates on the product packaging, especially on highly perishable items like cream.

DAY 1: Make sure that all crockery and cutlery are clean and ready for use.
Morning: Do the shopping according to your shopping list.
Afternoon: Make and freeze home-made ice cream.
Make sour cream dill sauce, cover and chill.
Arrange the flowers and set the tables.

DAY 2: Chill wine.
Morning: Prepare meat (don't cook) and chill.
Put out coffee cups, liqueur glasses and coffee machine.
Peel carrots, slice green beans in the French fashion and clean strawberries.Cover and refrigerate strawberries.
Squeeze fresh orange juice for the carrot dish.
Boil potatoes and pull off the skins.
Afternoon: Prepare and chill the salad.
Put out the serving dishes.
Switch on the hot trays (late afternoon).
Place the vegetables in the saucepans, ready to cook.
Cut the bread, place in baskets and cover.
Preheat the oven for cooking the meat.
Early evening: Place the meat in the oven.
Dish up the first course and place it on the table.
Finishing touches: Cook the vegetables, place in serving dishes and keep them warm on a hot tray.
Roast the potatoes.
Carve the meat and place on a hot tray.
Garnish the dishes.
Place the food on the table.

Preparation tips

When food is prepared on a large scale using a domestic oven, it is sometimes necessary to make certain adaptations or to employ specific methods. For example, some dishes must be baked one at a time, while others can quite happily be cooked together. Remember:

☐ Bake *dishes with a topping* (e.g. bobotie) separately – the egg layer is sensitive to overheating. In a convection oven, however, you can make two or more dishes of bobotie at the same time.
☐ Place a *dish with a mashed potato topping* 100 mm below the element, to brown it. Such dishes are cooked separately.
☐ You can bake two or more dishes of *lasagne* or *moussaka* at the same time.
☐ *Dishes having a batter* must cook evenly and are therefore placed in the oven separately.
☐ When grilling *sosaties* or *kebabs*, place them, in a single layer, 100 mm below the element. (Cover grilled sosaties with aluminium foil and keep them warm in a warming drawer.)

Casseroles

☐ More than one dish can be put in the oven, even if they have a dumpling topping.
☐ Place the dishes on different racks. Remember not to position the oven racks too close together, as this will work against the circulation of hot air.
☐ It's not necessary to adapt the oven temperature when increasing the number of servings.
☐ If you don't have large ceramic casserole dishes, use deep ovenproof dishes for your casserole. Cover with aluminium foil. (Some cast-iron saucepans can go in the oven, lid and all.)
☐ When making a casserole in a domestic oven, it's preferable to rotate the dishes during cooking – the middle of the oven is cooler than the area nearer to the element.
☐ Remember to brown meat before using it in a casserole.

Roasts

☐ More than one roasting cut (e.g. leg of lamb, fillet and rump) can be put in the oven at the same time. Place the meat on the rack of an oven-roasting pan. Remember to allow sufficient space between the meat cuts to allow air to circulate freely.
☐ Use one oven rack – you should be able to fit three roasts onto it.
☐ Choose roasts of about the same weight; the cooking time is calculated according to the average weight, and not according to the total weight.
☐ Choose meat cuts that are regular in shape to prevent thinner parts drying out during cooking.

Desserts

☐ Desserts should not, preferably, be placed too close to the element. You can place as many dishes as will fit on one rack into the oven at any one time.
☐ If you're using a deep ovenproof dish to bake a dessert, you may have to increase the baking time by up to 20 per cent (1 hour becomes 72 minutes, and so on). It could also be a good idea to leave the dessert in the oven for a short while after switching it off. Make sure that the dessert does not become too dark.

☐ Some ovens, after many years' use, are no longer as precisely calibrated as they should be. In such cases, it would be better to place desserts in the oven individually, to ensure that they cook evenly. Reheat the dessert before serving.
☐ Desserts baked in a water bath are not as vulnerable to temperature fluctuations because the hot water spreads the temperature evenly. More than one dish of such desserts (preferably in a single layer) can therefore be placed in the oven at one time.

Attractive presentation

Large serving dishes

If you don't often entertain large groups of people, it's unlikely that you will have large dishes and bowls in your kitchen cupboards. Here are a few ideas to help you circumvent the problem:

☐ For informal occasions, the saucepan in which the dish was cooked can be used for serving. Black cast-iron pots are particularly suitable. Make sure, however, that the rims of the saucepans are clean.
☐ Stews and the starch dish that goes with them can be served in black three-legged pots.
☐ For informal get-togethers, salads can be served on trays. Line the edges of the trays with lettuce or fresh herbs. A wooden tray looks particularly attractive.
☐ Use a fruit basket to serve rolls.
☐ One-dish meals can be made in deep baking dishes and served straight from the dishes. Make a nest of ivy or foliage to camouflage the dishes.
☐ Use flat planters for salad. Clay or ceramic containers look particularly good.
☐ Deep terracotta planters can be used as wine coolers.
☐ Copper dishes and trays used as ornaments make attractive containers for curries. Do not spoon the food directly into the dishes, but into containers that fit into them – the acid in the curries could react with the copper.

Garnishing

Even the simplest dish tastes better if it is attractively presented, so make the effort to liven up your food and make it look as good as possible. Here are a few garnishing ideas:

☐ Harmony and balance are important. Garnishes should round off the dish, never dominate it – keep it simple!
☐ Be creative when putting together a plate of food. Use different colours, textures and shapes. Alternate hot and cold dishes.
☐ One of the prerequisites for an attractive plate of food is fresh, healthy products. They have the perfect colour, texture and shape and are appealing to the eye.
☐ Vegetables are often self-garnishing. Glaze carrots to enhance the orange colour. Cut vegetables in bite-sized, rather than small, pieces. Use small, whole vegetables if possible – for example, young mealies, cherry tomatoes, pickling onions or baby carrots. Although these vegetables are often more expensive than the larger ones, the waste factor is also reduced. When baby carrots or baby beets are available with stalks, leave about 2 cm still attached – it looks most attractive.
☐ Dips to accompany raw vegetables can be served in a hollowed-out cabbage.
☐ Pickles can be served in an attractive preserving jar.
☐ Use fresh herbs and edible flowers to decorate hot and cold dishes. The herbs can be in bunches, sprigs or individual leaves, or finely chopped. A large pot roast or a whole chicken, for example, would be garnished with a bunch of herbs, and a fillet or portion of fish with a single sprig. Don't place herbs on hot food a long time before serving – they will wilt. Choose the herbs that best suit the food (see the box on p. 14).
☐ Garnish salads with a variety of chopped herbs, or place sprigs of fresh herbs between ingredients.
☐ Croutons, crisply fried bacon cubes or toasted nuts add to the appearance and flavour of salads and vegetables.
☐ Salad can be served on individual plates or in dishes.
☐ Perk up a cream sauce by adding chopped fresh parsley or a pinch of paprika. A drop of meat browning, on a knife-point, can be stirred in to make darker stripes in the sauce.
☐ Grated cheese, croutons or chopped herbs will add colour to a hot soup.
☐ Soup can be served in a hollowed-out pumpkin.

Above left: Mini lamb kebabs with mint sauce (p. 83).
Above right: Pumpkin with ginger syrup (p. 69).
Front: Stuffed whole chicken with Ham and mushroom stuffing (p. 82), served with Buttered young green beans (menu, p. 22).

HERBS AND SPICES

Fish
Bay leaves, rosemary, tarragon, dill, fennel, basil, lemon thyme and parsley are suitable for fish.

Veal
Marjoram and thyme are particularly suitable for veal because they complement the fairly neutral flavour. Use also star anise, basil, dill, tarragon, chervil, coriander, rosemary, sage, lemon balm, lemon thyme, fennel and parsley.

Lamb and mutton
Rosemary remains a favourite served with lamb. Use basil and marjoram with roasts, for delicious results. Try, too, savory, tarragon, bay leaves, sage, mint and parsley.

Pork
Sage is the most popular herb for pork. Use it sparingly, because the flavour can be overpowering. Star anise, basil, savory, dill, tarragon, chervil, coriander, mint, marjoram, rosemary, lemon balm, lemon thyme and fennel can also be used.

Chicken
Use basil, bay leaves, rosemary, dill, marjoram, fennel, lemon thyme and parsley in chicken dishes.

Beef
The following herbs are popular, especially if a little wine is added: basil, savory, tarragon, bay leaves, marjoram, rosemary, sage and parsley.

☐ An interesting way to serve hot soup is to cover the soup dishes with puff pastry and, just before serving, to bake it at 200 °C (400 °F) until golden brown and cooked.

☐ When making pies, use an implement with an interesting pattern to decorate the edges of the pastry. Cut out pastry shapes to place on top of the pie. Brush the pastry with beaten egg before baking. (Remember to use a pastry funnel or to make a slit in the pastry so that steam can escape during baking.)

☐ Make desserts in individual dishes – it looks so much neater than serving from a large dish.

☐ Garnish desserts with hibiscus, nasturtiums or rose petals. Grated lemon peel or even caramelised orange peel (with chocolate mousse) looks attractive.

☐ Be wary of using too much cream; rich desserts are no longer as popular. If cream is used, decorate it with chocolate pieces, cocoa or fresh fruit (strawberries or kiwi fruit, for instance). And don't forget the simple but classic mint sprig with a violet.

☐ Garnish fresh fruit desserts by sifting a little icing sugar over them, through a tea strainer. Dark baked puddings can also be decorated like this.

☐ Serve fruit salad in a glass dish with a foot. Decorate with mint leaves or granadilla pulp. Serve custard or cream separately.

☐ Fruit salad looks particularly appetising if the ingredients are grouped together in a shallow, square glass vase. For formal occasions, fruit salad can be arranged on top of a fruit purée on individual dessert plates, and garnished with mint leaves and violets.

☐ Fruit salad can also be served in a hollowed-out watermelon.

☐ Fruit dipped in a sugar syrup or melted chocolate (friandises) end an elegant dinner gracefully.

☐ To give fruit a frosted look, dip them in egg white and then in castor sugar. Place on a drying rack to allow the egg white to dry.

☐ Cheese and biscuits look good on a wooden or silver platter, with green or black grapes. Glacé fruit, figs for instance, can also be placed on the platter.

☐ Arrange chocolate on a silver platter or sparkling clean glass dish, without a doilie. Garnish with a few flowers. Chocolate can also be served with fresh fruit dipped in melted chocolate, or violets dipped in egg whites and castor sugar.

☐ Use a wooden serving spoon when a dish is presented in a rough ceramic, wood or copper container.

☐ Vine leaves and vineyard baskets look rustic and are suitable for informal occasions. Use deep red, green and dark blue accessories with wood and checked table linen. Tie checked ribbon around the baskets.

☐ Make an interesting base for serving strawberries, grapes or fruit balls. Freeze water and flowers, layer by layer, in a container to make an ice block. Unmould it by dipping it in boiling water for a few minutes. Place fruit or ice cream on top just before serving. (Serve immediately. Place the ice block on a tray or in a glass dish, for when the ice starts to melt.)

☐ Make sure that you have a pepper mill on the table, for guests to grind their own pepper. As an interesting variation, have green, pink and black peppercorns in the mill.

☐ If a simple white or plain coloured plate is used, a multi-coloured underplate will provide the contrast needed. Desserts can also be placed on a small plate on top of an hors d'oeuvres plate for an elegant and tasteful look.

Drinks

Remember

Your budget usually determines the variety of alcoholic drinks that will be offered. Order the liquor at least a week before the time. Remember to provide ice, corkscrews, a bath full of ice to keep drinks cold, and nonalcoholic drinks. Also arrange for the delivery of drink.

Make sure that you have enough glasses for the planned drinks. If you don't, you can hire them from large bottle stores. Find out what the conditions for hiring them are; for example, if glasses must be returned clean. Always make provision for breakages.

A separate table can be used for drinks. Position this table far away from the food table to avoid disturbing the traffic flow. Appoint someone to help pour the drinks.

How much drink will you need for 12 people?

White wine: 1 glass (150 ml) per person: 3 bottles
2 glasses per person: 6 bottles
Provide a dry and a semi-sweet white wine

Red wine: 1 glass (150 ml) per person: 3 bottles
2 glasses per person: 6 bottles

Beer: 1-2 dozen

Cool drinks 1 glass (250 ml) each: 3 litres
2 glasses each: 6 litres

Mineral water: 200 ml per person: 2,5 litres
2 glasses each: 6 litres

For a full wet bar, allow:

☐ Gin, whisky, brandy, sherry, port, martini, cane spirit.
☐ Liqueurs (2-3 kinds) and cognac.
☐ Soda water, tonic, other mixers, lemon slices and olives.

Serving drinks

☐ At informal get-togethers it isn't always necessary to provide separate glasses for white and red wine, but when it's a formal or semi-formal occasion, you will have to provide a glass for red wine, one for white wine and one for water. Liqueur, sherry and champagne glasses must also be provided if these drinks are to be served.

☐ Provide enough extra glasses for cool drinks, wine and alcoholic drinks to be enjoyed before the meal so that it won't be necessary to remove glasses from the already-set tables. For informal occasions, especially lap suppers, fewer glasses are needed. It's a good rule of thumb to allow the number of guests plus 50 per cent extra. (People often forget where they've left their drinks, especially at a braai or an informal do.)

☐ At formal affairs, have waiters to serve drinks to guests. You could have the waiters stationed at the door to welcome your guests with sherry or champagne, and have them serve guests liqueurs after the dessert as well as the coffee. Instruct some of the waiters to remove dirty glasses only, while others only serve drinks. This avoids guests being confronted with dirty glasses and drinks on the same tray.

☐ Drinks served at table at a formal affair are poured from behind the guest's right shoulder. If both red and white wine are available, they should be offered to guests at the same time. Cold water is automatically provided for each guest at formal dinners. If you prefer, you can offer specific wines with each course, for example:

Fish starter – white wine
Red meat dish – red wine (full-bodied)
Sweet dessert – port
Coffee and chocolate – liqueurs

☐ Guests can pour their own drinks at informal get-togethers. The host will have to keep a weather eye on the supplies, however, to make sure that there's enough of everything.

More tips

☐ The hostess generally knows her guests well and knows how much provision she needs to make for drinks. Women generally drink less than men, and you can, therefore, adjust quantities according to the ratio of men to women. Remember, too, how many children there will be, and their ages. Consult your local bottle store for more information.

☐ If some of your guests are dedicated drinkers, make provision for this by finding out what they drink and purchasing sufficient stocks.

☐ If a hot meal is to be served on a cold evening, "glühwein" will make an excellent appetiser.

☐ For hot evenings, make margaritas or cocktails and decorate them festively with glacé cherries, orange or pineapple slices.

☐ If you have a good wine cellar, spoil your guests with a rare vintage.

☐ Make sure that the red wine is opened early enough to allow it plenty of time to breathe.

☐ Use attractive decanters for sherry and port.

☐ For informal occasions, decant boxed wine into glass decanters. Wine of a good vintage, however, is never decanted into another container.

The venue

Seating

Prepare the traffic and sitting areas for the number of guests expected. Make sure that access to these areas is easy and remove free-standing breakables to prevent the embarrassment of accidental breakage. Seating arranged in smaller conversation groups creates a cosy atmosphere; large cushions can be used here and there for an informal affair. Make sure that there are enough small tables for putting down drinks, as glasses placed on the floor or next to a chair can easily be knocked over. Provide helpers to remove dirty glasses and ashtrays and to replace the latter with clean ones. Position flowers where they will have the greatest impact, but not be in the way. Place snacks where guests can reach them easily.

Dining areas (sit-down meals)

The size and shape of the dining room will determine the number of tables and their shape. Depending on the number of guests, they can sit at just one table, or at a number of smaller tables. It would be preferable to have six, eight or ten at a table, depending on the size of the group. Round tables often provide a more informal atmosphere (especially if they are small), while long tables are more suitable for formal occasions. It is much more difficult to conduct a conversation across a large table, because people cannot always hear one another. Make sure, therefore, that the background music is not too loud.

If you have a large group to entertain, and want to use one large table, long tables can be arranged in an L-, U- or T-shape. All the guests will be sitting at the same table. This is sometimes the only solution if space is at a premium. The disadvantage of such an arrangement of tables is that a guest can only converse with the people on either side of, and directly opposite, him. It can also be a bit cramped.

If your dining room is too small, you could hire a marquee and put it up in the garden. This creates a most festive atmosphere and the placing of tables is seldom a problem. Do, however, make sure that the tables are standing securely, and that there aren't any hidden holes in the lawn. The poles of the marquee can be decorated with net and climbers.

Setting the table

Place cards and menus

Remember to provide place cards and menus for each table. Place cards make guests feel important and welcome, and make it easier for them to mix, especially at formal occasions where they don't all know one another. Keep the place cards and menus simple and functional – don't overdecorate them. At formal affairs, a menu is placed on each table, but a menu on the buffet table is sufficient for informal occasions.

Table linen

The table linen used will depend on the kind of occasion, the shape of the tables and the availability of linen. It's more usual to use white table linen – for example, brocade – for a formal meal, but there are few rules regarding colour and texture for an informal get-together. Brightly coloured tablecloths and serviettes brighten everything up – especially in winter – and will be suited to a menu featuring stews or curry. Cool pastel colours are ideal for summer. Place mats can also be used for informal meals.

Flowers

Flowers on the tables must match the table linen. Use pot plants with brightly coloured flowers instead of an arrangement, which requires a lot of time to make. Arrange flowers in a flat, or very high, container so that guests sitting opposite one another can communicate. Make sure that the flowers do not take up too large a part of the table, leaving no place for the cutlery.

Cutlery and glasses

Always make sure that all cutlery and glasses have been buffed to sparkling perfection before placing them on the table. The cutlery needed is determined by the occasion: at an informal affair, like a braai where guests eat on their laps, knives and forks can simply be wrapped in serviettes.

At a sit-down dinner, the dishes usually determine the kind and number of cutlery items. For the first course, the cutlery required is usually a spoon for soup (placed with the knives), or a small knife and fork (or fish knife and fork), for something like salmon trout, for instance. A bread knife is placed on the side plate, or with the other knives. The main course knife and fork are placed to the inside of the small knife and fork, followed by the dessert spoon (with the knives) and fork. The cutlery for the different courses works from the outside in, as the meal progresses.

The wineglasses are placed in a straight line above the large knives. The red wine glass is on the outside, followed by a white wine glass and a water glass. Glasses can also be arranged from left to right, diagonally or in a triangle. These strict rules for place settings apply mostly to formal occasions.

Serviettes

Serviettes can be placed on the side plate (if bread is to be served) with the bread knife on top, or folded in an interesting way and placed between the knife and fork. Watch out for too flamboyant folds – they can look overdone. Simplicity is always better. Paper serviettes are only used at very informal get-togethers, and should not be placed in glasses.

Salt and pepper

Provide sufficient salt and pepper shakers for each table. For formal occasions, each guest – or every two guests – should have a cruet set. Providing these ensures that guests don't have to ask or lean over other guests to get the salt.

Ashtrays
You don't have to place ashtrays on the tables, but perhaps the best course of action would be not to put ashtrays on the table for the main part of the meal – this discourages guests from smoking between courses and offending other guests. Have ashtrays at hand to place on the table when the coffee is served. Ensure that there are enough clean ashtrays, so that a dirty one can always be replaced by a clean one.

Bread, butter and salad
Although it's not the norm to place any food on a formal table, bread and butter can sometimes be put there. When the occasion is semi-formal, a number of smaller dishes of salad can also be placed on the table, but it would be best not to adopt this practice.

The serving area
Decoration
Apart from providing seating for guests, provision must also be made for a serving area for the food. The decoration of this area is the prelude to the meal: use flowers, candles and colourful tablecloths to create the appropriate atmosphere. Vary the height at which dishes are placed on the service tables, by placing them on cardboard boxes. Use interesting containers, in different shapes, and in colours that match the table linen.

Planning
☐ The serving area should be planned in such a way that it makes the traffic flow more easily. Place plates at the start, followed by hot dishes and salad. The area can also be divided so that the first course (if not placed on the tables), main course, dessert, coffee and drinks are on separate tables.
☐ The buffet table is set as
from start to finish):

– Plates
– Meat dishes
– Vegetables, starch dishes and gravies
– Salads and dressings
– Trays, cutlery and serviettes

The first course and dessert should be served on separate tables, if possible. When there are 12 or more guests, you could consider having more than two service stations. Serving will also be much better if the tables are placed in the centre of the room in a T-shape.
☐ There must be sufficient ovenproof dishes (preferably with lids) for keeping food warm. Provide enough hot trays too, and make sure that they are switched on in plenty of time. Note the position of power points and get extension cords where necessary.
☐ Make provision for one or two people to help with service at a buffet table. These people can be of help with the main course in particular – which also helps control the portion sizes.
☐ Make sure that there are enough serving spoons, meat forks and salad spoons (at least two of each for each dish).
☐ An informal table can be set with all the cutlery, trays (if people are going to eat on their laps), crockery and food.
☐ For an outdoor afternoon function, make provision for umbrellas if there are not enough shade trees. The food table, in particular, should be in shade to prevent wilting and spoiling. All perishables should be placed on the table just before serving.
☐ Coffee after the meal is optional at informal parties. A Thermos flask of coffee, milk and/or cream and sugar can be placed on a separate table for self-service. Coffee mugs are suitable for this. Formal and semi-formal meals are usually followed by coffee. This can be served at table, or after the guests have left the table.

Service methods

Informal occasions
Service can take a number of forms. Depending on the number of guests, all dishes can be placed on one table, or the starter, main course and dessert can be placed on separate tables. Cutlery is placed on the table with the food. Bread, butter, salt and pepper can be placed on the tables in advance. Guests can dish up for themselves, but it's usually a good idea to have at least one person to help with the serving of the meat course. Guests can then – depending on the available space or the hostess's preference – eat on their laps or at tables. (It's also a good idea to allow guests to decide for themselves where they want to eat. Make sure that there is enough seating, and enough trays, for those who want to eat on their laps.)

Semi-formal occasions
Guests generally sit down at a table for such meals, but the service can still be buffet style. First courses can be placed on the tables in advance; waiters can remove the plates and cutlery for the first course while the main course is being served. The dessert can be served from a separate buffet table. While the dessert is being dished up, all the cutlery, empty glasses and cruet sets are removed from the table. Coffee and chocolate can be served at table, or after guests have left the table.

Formal occasions
Here it is the custom to serve all the courses at table. One waiter per eight guests is usually sufficient; preferably they should be trained waiters or well-instructed school children. Waiters and other helpers must be told, in advance, what the order of dishes is to be. Doing this means that the hostess doesn't have to scurry around between kitchen and table. Dishes are thus dished up in advance, and guests only help themselves to bread and butter. Salad can also be served individually or

per table. Sufficient kitchen help is essential for this kind of service; if necessary, a chef can be hired for the evening.

Remember: At a formal function, empty plates are removed from the right, and the next course is put down on the table from the left side.

More things to do

See also *Planning is essential, Drinks, The venue,* and *The serving area.*

The guest list

Draw up a guest list at least three to four weeks before the event. It's important to invite people with common interests, occupation or background, at the same time.

As soon as you have decided on the number of guests and invited them, you can draw up a preliminary seating plan. Remember to seat men and women alternately around the table, and not to place couples together – in this way new friendships are forged. If necessary, you can arrange now for the making of place cards and menus.

Invitations

All invitations should contain the following information: the kind of occasion, how formal it is, the date, the time, and an RSVP date. This should be at least ten days before the party date, to allow you to amend plans if necessary.

How you invite guests depends on how well you know them. Good friends and old acquaintances are more often invited to informal occasions and can be invited by phone or by an informal card. Answer cards aren't necessary, but do ask for a reply by a certain date.

Keep a list of invited guests nearby, and mark off the names as you receive replies. For informal affairs, if you haven't heard from guests by a certain date, simply phone them. If you're sending invitation cards, make provision for some of them getting lost in the post. It is thus important to follow up unanswered invitations in plenty of time, in case the invitation didn't reach its destination. Always have a few extra cards printed to allow for unforeseen circumstances.

A printed or beautifully written invitation is best for a formal occasion. Include an answer card with your full address, the RSVP date and a stamp on it. Post the invitations; in special cases, you can have them delivered by messenger.

If invitations are sent well in advance, you can send a reminder. Repeat all the relevant information so that the problem of lost invitations can be solved at the same time.

Another venue

If your home is not large enough, you will have to find a suitable venue – in plenty of time. Remember that there should be power points and, if possible, a kitchen adjoining the venue. If the venue doesn't have such facilities, hire or borrow gas plates to keep dishes hot. The menu should then be chosen in such a way that it requires the minimum oven space and space for keeping warm. Consider, too, the available cooling facilities.

Hiring

For a sit-down function, it's often necessary to hire tables and chairs. The number of guests will determine whether everyone can sit at one table, or whether there should be a number of tables for 6-8 or 8-12 guests.

Make sure that you have enough tablecloths, serviettes, cutlery and crockery. These articles are available on hire from various firms in large cities. In the country, you could perhaps hire them from the local church, or borrow them from your friends. Remember always to order 10 per cent more plates, to allow for breakages. Take note of the hiring conditions with regard to returns and breakages.

If you have a small dining room but a large garden, you could consider hiring a marquee for very special occasions. Alternatively, you could plan an alfresco meal in the afternoon, but you will need umbrellas if you do not have enough shade trees.

Lighting

Sufficient lighting is essential if you are having an alfresco party in the evening. Flares are attractive and, at the same time, offer sufficient light for guests to see where they are walking. They should also be able to see clearly what is being offered to eat. Remember that light attracts insects – so provide a net to cover the food on the table before the meal.

Music

The occasion will determine the music. If musicians are hired, they should be booked at least three weeks beforehand (popular musicians often even longer in advance). Remember that there are many weddings and year-end parties in spring and summer and that bookings for these busy periods must be made well in advance.

Parking

If possible, for a function at home, arrange with neighbours that guests can park on their property. It could also be a good idea to get someone to show guests where to park – this will prevent their parking on forbidden areas. The security of parking is an important factor if you are having the function elsewhere, and you have a choice of venue. It could also be necessary to hire a guard to look after cars while the guests are at the function.

Toilets

Before the party, make sure that the toilet facilities are clean and tidy. If there is more than one toilet, it would be a good idea to allocate one for men and one for women. Remember to provide soap, clean towels and extra toilet paper. If you are entertaining a very large group of people, it may be necessary to check later in the evening that there are still sufficient supplies. A bunch of flowers and hand cream always look attractive, and a bowl of potpourri adds the final touch.

Flowers

Flowers always create a festive atmosphere. Simply by well-considered use of flowers, the hostess can put her stamp on the occasion and create a special atmosphere. Place a few large arrangements in appropriate places – for example, near the front door and serving areas. Smaller bouquets can be placed strategically – on the tables, for instance, or with the dessert. Flowers used as garnishes for food must be edible: rose petals, hibiscus leaves and nasturtiums are safe.

Order or make arrangements to obtain flowers and their containers in plenty of time. When flowers are expensive (during the winter months), use foliage or plants with berries. Ivy wreaths offer an interesting alternative. Ivy can also be placed between the serving dishes or fastened around the tablecloths.

Washing up

To prevent the piling up of dirty dishes, make sure well in advance that you will have people to wash dishes for the duration of the function. Hired plates sometimes come in holders that can also be used as drying racks. Glasses should be washed and dried as soon as possible, so that there are always clean glasses.

If the occasion is informal, you could ask a friend or your daughter to help remove plates, scrape them clean and stack them neatly. Never try to wash the dishes yourself, in between everything else!

Rubbish

Make sure that you have enough rubbish bins and black bags to allow you to throw food scraps, cans and cigarette ends away immediately. Provide a cardboard box for packing empty bottles as well. Keep the rubbish area tidy at all times, and out of sight of guests. The people enlisted to help serve the food, should be fully informed about the procedure for handling rubbish, leftovers and dirty dishes.

Accidents

Make sure that you know how to remove various stains; it could save a guest a good deal of embarrassment – not to mention prevent damage. Always act in a relaxed manner if there is such an accident, to put guests at their ease.

You and your guests

The welcome

☐ When guests arrive at a function, the hostess and host receive them at the door. The host can then accompany the new arrivals to a group of guests, introduce them and explain where and how the drinks are served.

☐ On formal occasions, it is important to know the titles and names of people. This is particularly important when you do not know the spouses of guests personally; make sure that you know how to address them.

☐ Remain formal until such time as the guest asks you to use his or her Christian name. This is generally not a problem at informal parties.

☐ When introducing one guest to others, it is a good idea to give a short background to that guest. The other guests will immediately feel more comfortable and the conversation will also flow more easily if people have a common interest.

☐ It is essential, at formal occasions, to provide each guest with a seating plan when he or she arrives. This prevents an unnecessary scurrying around before the meal starts.

☐ Guests often bring a small gift for the hostess. Accept it with thanks; a follow-up letter to thank the guest is not necessary. Make sure that there is someone to take the gift from you, especially if it's flowers which need to be put in water immediately.

☐ A single rose or a small gift is sometimes given to women guests at formal functions. It would be better to hand these over at the end of the evening, otherwise they have to carry it around with them all evening.

At table

The hostess must look relaxed at all times. Leave enough time between courses to avoid a hurried atmosphere, but don't take too long to serve the food, especially if it is a dinner.

The hostess excuses herself when the guests have almost finished eating, and the dessert is dished up or served buffet style. Depending on the number of people and the occasion, guests can then be invited into the sitting room for coffee and liqueurs.

Pack away only those items that are perishable. Leave the table as it is, covered with net, because the hostess's place is with her guests.

Pocket-wise menus

The menus in this section are intended for those stony-broke months when it seems that sandwiches and cold water are all you can afford. These economical, tasty dishes will enable you to entertain with confidence – and no one will guess that you're short on cash! They are also eminently suitable for the kinds of meals arranged by schools, churches or welfare organisations with the aim of raising funds. Read on – there are ideas to suit every pocket and taste.

Above left: Yellow rice with raisins (menu, p. 24). Above right: Minted peas (menu, p. 28). Bottom from left: Dried fruit in rooibos tea (p. 24); Bobotie (p. 24) and Curried fish (p. 31).

Beef casserole

Ingredients	12 servings	24 servings	48 servings
Beef bolo, thick rib or topside, cut into 25 mm cubes	1,5 kg	3 kg	6 kg
Cooking oil	30 ml	80 ml	150 ml
Medium onions, sliced	300 g (3)	500 g (5)	1 kg (10)
Garlic cloves, crushed	2	3	5
Cake flour	90 ml (45 g)	180 ml (85 g)	375 ml (180 g)
Salt	7 ml	15 ml	30 ml
Freshly ground black pepper	2 ml	4 ml	8 ml
Potatoes, cubed	450 g (3)	900 g (6)	1,8 kg (12)
Carrots, sliced	300 g (3)	500 g (5)	1 kg (10)
Tomatoes, skinned and sliced	360 g (3)	720 g (6)	1,4 kg (12)
Meat stock	350 ml	750 ml	1,5 litres

Preparation

- ☐ Cube the meat.
- ☐ Peel and slice the onions.
- ☐ Peel and crush the garlic cloves.
- ☐ Peel and cube the potatoes.
- ☐ Peel and slice the carrots.
- ☐ Skin and slice the tomatoes.

Method

Brown the meat in heated oil in a heavy-based saucepan. Add the onions and garlic and sauté until translucent. Spoon the meat into a large casserole dish. Mix the flour and seasonings thoroughly. Layer the meat and vegetables and sprinkle the flour mixture over. Pour the heated meat stock over the meat, cover and bake for 1½-2 hours in a preheated oven at 160 °C (325 °F), or until the meat is tender. Add more liquid during cooking, if necessary.

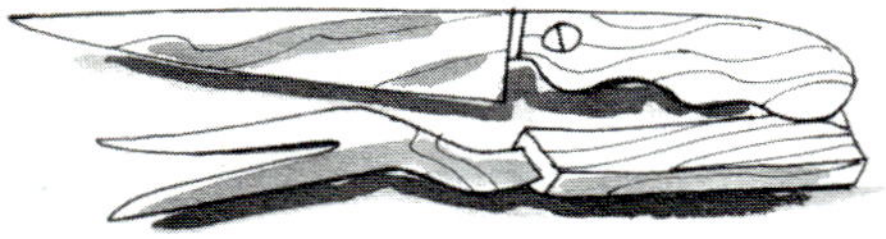

Variations

Batter-topped casserole

(48 servings; use ¼ or ½ of the quantities for 12 or 24 servings)

1 litre milk
1 litre cooking oil
8 eggs, beaten
1 kg cake flour (8 x 250 ml + 80 ml)
80 ml baking powder
15 ml salt
3 onions, cut into slices

Method

Beat the milk, oil and eggs together thoroughly. Sift the dry ingredients together and mix them to a smooth batter with the milk mixture. Pour over the cooked casserole, place onion slices on top of the batter and bake for 20 minutes, uncovered, at 180 °C (350 °F) or until golden brown and cooked.

Dumplings

(48 servings; use ¼ or ½ of the quantities for 12 or 24 servings)

750 g cake flour (6 x 250 ml + 60 ml)
75 ml baking powder
20 ml salt
800 ml milk
100 ml chopped fresh parsley or mixed herbs (optional)

Method

Sift the dry ingredients together. Add the milk and mix to a smooth batter. Add the parsley or mixed herbs, if desired. Drop spoonfuls on top of the casserole, cover and return to the oven for a further 20 minutes.

Menu

Clear vegetable soup with croutons*

Beef casserole* with dumplings*
Buttered young green beans
Green salad with French dressing*

Baked brown pudding with caramel custard*

For 12 people you will need:

- ☐ 2,4 litres vegetable soup
- ☐ 1,2 kg green beans
- ☐ salad ingredients:
  - *1 medium cucumber*
  - *1 medium lettuce*
  - *2 medium green sweet peppers*
  - *3 small avocados*
  - *1 small onion*

Topside curry

Ingredients	12 servings	24 servings	48 servings
Beef topside, cut into 25 mm cubes	1,8 kg	3 kg	5,5 kg
Cooking oil	40 ml	80 ml	150 ml
Medium onions, finely chopped	300 g (3)	500 g (5)	1 kg (10)
Mild curry powder	15 g	30 g	60 g
Turmeric	5 g	10 g	20 g
Meat stock	500 ml	1 litre	2 litres
Tomato paste	60 g	125 g	250 g
Vinegar	125 ml	250 ml	500 ml
Apricot jam	125 ml	250 ml	500 ml
Salt	10 ml	20 ml	40 ml
Freshly ground black pepper	4 ml	8 ml	15 ml
Potatoes, cubed	750 g (5)	1,5 kg (10)	3 kg (20)
Cake flour	50 ml (25 g)	100 ml (50 g)	200 ml (100 g)

Preparation
- ☐ Cube the meat.
- ☐ Peel and chop the onions.
- ☐ Peel and cube the potatoes.

Method
Brown the meat in heated oil in a heavy-based saucepan. Add the onions and sauté until translucent. Add the curry powder and turmeric and fry for a few minutes. Add the heated stock, tomato paste, vinegar, apricot jam and seasonings. Reduce the heat, cover and simmer for 1½-2 hours or until the meat is almost tender. Add the potato cubes and simmer for a further 30 minutes. Thicken gravy with flour mixed to a paste with water.

Tip
☐ Boned lamb thick rib cubes can be used instead of topside. Bay leaves can be added for extra flavour.

Tomato sambal

(12 servings; use 2 or 4 times the quantities for 24 or 48 servings)

4 ripe tomatoes, cubed
1 onion, finely chopped
salt and pepper to taste
50 ml lemon juice
15 ml sugar

Method
Mix all the ingredients thoroughly and serve chilled.

Variations
Cucumber sambal: Use ½ English cucumber, grated, instead of tomatoes. Add 175 ml natural yoghurt to the rest of the ingredients and mix thoroughly.
Sweet pepper sambal: Use 2 red and 3 green sweet peppers, seeded and finely chopped, instead of tomatoes. Follow the instructions for tomato sambal.

Menu

Topside curry*
White rice
Tomato sambal*
Cucumber sambal*
Chutney
Coconut

Lemon sorbet with litchis

For 12 people you will need:
- ☐ 400 g rice
- ☐ 360 ml chutney
- ☐ 90 ml coconut
- ☐ 1,2 litres lemon sorbet
- ☐ 500 g canned or fresh stoned litchis (without syrup)

Bobotie

Ingredients	12 servings	24 servings	48 servings
Minced beef	1,5 kg	3 kg	6 kg
Medium onions, chopped	400 g (4)	800 g (8)	1,5 kg (15)
Cooking oil	15 ml	30 ml	50 ml
Mild curry powder	40 ml (25 g)	80 ml (50 g)	160 ml (100 g)
Turmeric	20 ml (12 g)	40 ml (25 g)	80 ml (50 g)
Grape vinegar	50 ml	100 ml	200 ml
Smooth apricot jam	50 ml (90 g)	100 ml (180 g)	200 ml (350 g)
White bread slices	3 (90 g)	6 (180 g)	12 (350 g)
Milk	80 ml	150 ml	300 ml
Salt	7 ml	15 ml	30 ml
Freshly ground black pepper	1 ml	3 ml	5 ml
Eggs	4	8	16
Milk	400 ml	750 ml	1,5 litres
Bay leaves or lemon leaves	8	10	16

Preparation

☐ Chop the onions and sauté them in heated oil until translucent. Add the curry powder and turmeric and fry for a few minutes. Add the vinegar and apricot jam and simmer for 2 minutes. Allow to cool.

☐ Soak the bread in the milk.

Method

Squeeze the milk lightly from the bread and mash the bread. Mix the meat, curry mixture, bread and seasonings lightly, using 2 forks. Place the meat mixture in ovenproof dishes. Beat the eggs and milk together (including the milk squeezed from the bread). Press funnel-shaped bay or lemon leaves here and there into the meat mixture. Pour the egg mixture over the meat. Bake the bobotie for 30-40 minutes in a preheated oven at 160 °C (325 °F) or until the egg mixture has set.

Dried fruit in rooibos tea

(12 servings; use 2 or 4 times the quantities for 24 or 48 servings, but 1½ or 3 times the quantity of rooibos tea)

2 kg mixed dried fruit
3 litres rooibos tea
60 ml brown sugar
30 ml lemon juice
6 whole cloves
3 cinnamon sticks

Method

Soak the dried fruit for 2-3 hours in the rooibos tea.

Add the brown sugar, lemon juice, whole cloves and cinnamon sticks and simmer for 30-40 minutes or until the fruit is tender. Serve with the bobotie.

Braised green beans

(12 servings; use 2 or 4 times the quantities for 24 or 48 servings)

2 medium onions, finely chopped
10 ml butter
1,2 kg green beans, thinly sliced
2 medium potatoes, sliced
2 medium tomatoes, skinned and cubed
100 g smoked pork, diced
100 ml meat stock
salt and pepper to taste

Method

Sauté the onions in heated butter until translucent. Add the rest of the ingredients, except the salt and pepper, and simmer for 40 minutes or until the vegetables are tender. Mash with a fork and season with salt and pepper to taste.

Menu

Bobotie*
Yellow rice with raisins
Dried fruit in rooibos tea*
Braised green beans*

Vinegar pudding*

For 12 people you will need:

☐ 400 g rice
☐ 60 g raisins

Bolognaise meat sauce

Ingredients	12 servings	24 servings	48 servings
Minced topside	1,8 kg	2,8 kg	6 kg
Cooking oil or olive oil	30 ml	75 ml	150 ml
Medium onions, chopped	300 g (3)	500 g (5)	1 kg (10)
Garlic cloves, crushed	5	10	18
Salt	10 ml	17 ml	25-30 ml
Freshly ground black pepper	3 ml	6 ml	10 ml
Dried or freshly chopped mixed herbs	7 ml or 20 ml	15 ml or 45 ml	30 ml or 90ml
Tomato purée	250 ml	500 ml	900 ml
Brown sugar	10 ml	20 ml	30 ml
Meat stock	750 ml	1,5 litres	3 litres
Cake flour	15 ml (5 g)	30 ml (15 g)	40-60 ml (20-30 g)

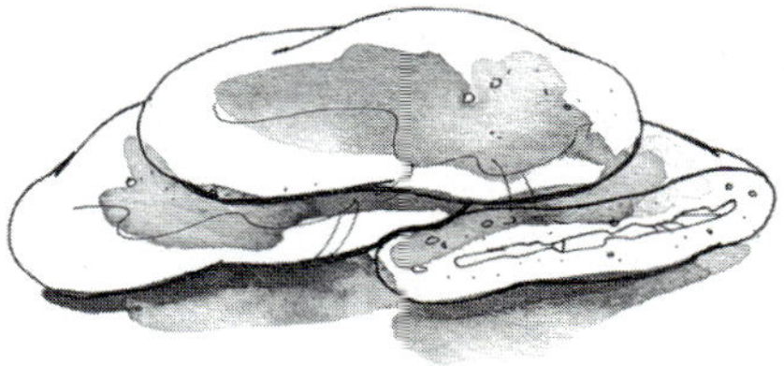

Preparation
☐ Peel and chop the onions.
☐ Peel and crush the garlic.

Method
Fry the mince in the heated oil in a heavy-based saucepan until it changes colour. Add the onions and garlic and sauté until translucent. Add the remaining ingredients, except the cake flour. Reduce the heat, cover with the lid and simmer for 30-45 minutes. Thicken the sauce with cake flour mixed to a paste with water.

Tip
☐ Bolognaise sauce can also be used as a filling for pancakes, potatoes or vetkoek.

Melon with smoked ham

(48 servings; use ¼ or ½ of the quantities for 12 or 24 servings)

6-7 winter melons, seeded and peeled
1,8 kg smoked ham, sliced paper-thin
6 lemons, cut into wedges

Method
Slice melon thinly, lengthways. Arrange two melon slices and smoked ham slices for each starter.

Garnish each plate with a lemon wedge and serve.

Menu

Melon with smoked ham*

Bolognaise meat sauce*
Spaghetti
Greek salad with olives
Pita bread with garlic butter

Natural yoghurt with honey and nuts

For 12 people you will need:
☐ 800 g spaghetti
☐ 40 g Parmesan cheese

The size of the saucepan will determine how much pasta can be cooked at one time. The secret is to allow a large quantity of boiling water for each batch. (Use 10 ml cooking oil per litre of water.) Serve the pasta immediately.

☐ salad ingredients:
1 medium lettuce
1 medium cucumber
3 medium tomatoes
1 small onion
250 g feta cheese
24 olives
☐ 12 pita breads
☐ 60 g garlic butter
☐ 2,1 litres natural yoghurt
☐ 120-150 ml honey
☐ 240 g nuts

Goulash

Ingredients	12 servings	24 servings	48 servings
Boned thick rib of beef, cut into 20 mm cubes	1,75 kg	3,5 kg	6,5 kg
Cooking oil	50 ml	100 ml	200 ml
Medium onions, chopped	300 g (3)	500 g (5)	1 kg (10)
Paprika	10 ml	15 ml	25 ml
Salt	10 ml	18 ml	25 ml
Freshly ground black pepper	3 ml	5 ml	10 ml
Tomato purée	250 ml	500 ml	800 ml
Meat stock	350 ml	600 ml	1,2 litres
Carrots, sliced	500 g (5)	1 kg (10)	2 kg (20)
Cake flour	30 ml (15 g)	60 ml (30 g)	125 ml (60 g)
Chopped fresh parsley	50 ml	100 ml	200 ml

Preparation

☐ Cube the meat.
☐ Peel the onions and carrots.
☐ Chop the onions finely and slice the carrots.
☐ Chop the parsley.

Method

Brown the meat in heated oil in a heavy-based saucepan. Add the onions and sauté until translucent. Add the seasoning, tomato purée and heated stock. Reduce the heat, cover with the lid and simmer for 1 hour or until the meat is almost tender. Add the carrots and simmer for a further 30-45 minutes. Thicken the gravy with the flour mixed to a paste with water. Garnish with chopped parsley.

Tip

☐ Bolo, topside, silverside or thick flank may be used instead of thick rib.

Menu

Fish soup*
Whole-wheat bread

Goulash*
Brown rice
Buttered peas and carrots

Milk tart

For 12 people you will need:

☐ 1 whole-wheat loaf (20 slices)
☐ 400 g brown rice
☐ 1,1 kg frozen peas
☐ 1,4 kg carrots
☐ 2 milk tarts, each 225 mm in diameter (150 g a serving)

Fish soup

(12 servings; use 2 or 4 times the quantities for 24 or 48 servings)

2 cans tuna, drained and flaked
2 cans (2 x 410 g) cream of tomato soup
2 cans (2 x 410 g) evaporated milk
salt and pepper to taste

Method

Mix all the ingredients and heat to boiling point. Serve with fresh whole-wheat bread.

Cottage pie

Ingredients	12 servings	24 servings	48 servings
Minced topside	2 kg	3,5 kg	5,5 kg
Cooking oil	15 ml	25 ml	50 ml
Medium onions, chopped	400 g (4)	700 g (7)	1,4 kg (14)
Garlic cloves, crushed	2	4	8
Salt	10 ml	15 ml	30 ml
Freshly ground black pepper	2 ml	4 ml	8 ml
Ground cloves	3 ml	8 ml	15 ml
Meat stock	700 ml	1,4 litres	2,6 litres
Tomato purée	150 ml	250 ml	500 ml
Cake flour	30 ml (15 g)	50 ml (25 g)	100 ml (50 g)
Mashed potato topping:			
Potatoes, peeled	600 g (4)	1,2 kg (8)	2,4 kg (16)
Grated nutmeg	2 ml	4 ml	8 ml
Milk	100 ml	200 ml	400 ml
Butter	40 g	80 g	150 g
Salt	4 ml	8 ml	15 ml

Preparation

☐ Peel and chop the onions.
☐ Peel and crush the garlic cloves.
☐ Boil the potatoes in water until tender. Drain.

Method

Fry the meat in heated oil in a heavy-based saucepan until it changes colour. Add the onions and garlic and sauté until translucent. Add the seasonings, heated stock and tomato purée. Reduce the heat, cover with the lid and simmer for 30 minutes. Thicken the gravy with the flour mixed to a paste with water.

Prepare the potato topping: Mash the potatoes, add the remaining ingredients and mix thoroughly.

Spoon the meat mixture into an ovenproof dish and spoon the potato mixture over. Bake for 20 minutes in a preheated oven at 180 °C (350 °F) or until golden brown.

Tips

☐ For feather-light mashed potatoes, add 10-15 ml baking powder to the potato mixture and mix well.
☐ Stir the mince with a fork while frying it to ensure a lump-free texture.

Baked cinnamon apples

(48 servings; use ¼ or ½ of the quantities for 12 or 24 servings)

48 Granny Smith or cooking apples
250 ml chopped nuts
250 ml brown sugar
250 ml sultanas or seedless raisins
125 ml lemon juice
250 g butter
48 cinnamon sticks

Method

Cut off the top of each apple. Core the apples, leaving the base intact. Fill the apples with nuts, brown sugar and sultanas. Sprinkle lemon juice over and dot each with butter. Place a cinnamon stick in each apple. Arrange them in an ovenproof dish. Pour boiling water into the ovenproof dish to 10 mm deep and bake for about 25 minutes at 180 °C (350 °F) until the apples are tender but still keep their shape. Serve with hot custard.

Menu

Cottage pie*
Buttered mixed green vegetables
Grilled tomatoes
Mixed green salad with onion rings

Baked cinnamon apples*

For 12 people you will need:

☐ 1,1 kg mixed green vegetables
☐ 12 medium tomatoes
☐ salad ingredients:
250 g young spinach leaves, stalks removed
1 medium cucumber
50 ml chopped parsley
240 g bean sprouts
2 small onions

Braised pork and apples

Ingredients	12 servings	24 servings	48 servings
Boned lean thick rib of pork, cut into 25 mm cubes	1,75 kg	3,5 kg	7 kg
Cooking oil	40 ml	75 ml	150 ml
Medium onions, finely chopped	200 g (2)	400 g (4)	800 g (8)
Apple juice	400 ml	800 ml	1,5 litres
Salt	10 ml	20 ml	50 ml
White pepper	3 ml	5 ml	10 ml
Cloves	3 ml	5 ml	10 ml
Cinnamon sticks	1	2	4
Soy sauce	25 ml	40 ml	80 ml
Sultanas	65 g	125 g	250 g
Cooking apples, cored and cubed	300 g (3)	500 g (5)	1 kg (10)
Cake flour	30 ml (15 g)	60 ml (30 g)	125 ml (50 g)

Menu

Braised pork and apples*
White rice with parsley
Minted peas
Buttered carrots

Baked bananas with cream*

For 12 people you will need:
- ☐ 400 g rice
- ☐ 1,1 kg frozen peas
- ☐ 1,4 kg carrots

Preparation
- ☐ Cube the meat.
- ☐ Peel and chop the onions.
- ☐ Core and cube the apples.

Method
Brown the meat in heated oil in a heavy-based saucepan. Add the onions and sauté until translucent. Add the heated apple juice, salt, pepper, cloves, cinnamon sticks, soy sauce and sultanas. Reduce the heat, cover with the lid and simmer for 1-1½ hours or until the meat is almost tender. Add the apples and simmer for a further 30 minutes. Thicken the gravy with the flour mixed to a paste with water.

Tips
- ☐ Use pineapple pieces and pineapple juice instead of cooking apples and apple juice.
- ☐ Instead of sultanas and cooking apples, use mixed dried fruit soaked in rooibos tea.

Baked bananas with cream

(12 servings; use 2 or 4 times the quantities for 24 or 48 servings)

12 ripe bananas, halved lengthways
30 ml lemon juice
60 ml brown sugar
60 ml coconut
30 ml butter

360 ml fresh cream

Method
Arrange the bananas in an ovenproof dish. Sprinkle the lemon juice over. Sprinkle the sugar and coconut over and dot with butter. Bake for 10-15 minutes at 180 °C (350 °F) or until golden brown. Serve with cream.

Above left: Beef casserole with dumplings (p. 22). Bottom from left: Buttered young green beans (menu, p. 22) and Green salad (menu, p. 22) with French dressing (p. 92).

Chicken and rice casserole

Ingredients	12 servings	24 servings	48 servings
Chicken portions (drumsticks, thighs or breasts)	12	24	48
Cooking oil	40 ml	75 ml	120 ml
Medium onions, cut into rings	400 g (4)	700 g (7)	1,2 kg (12)
Bacon, cubed	125 g	250 g	500 g
White rice (uncooked)	125 g	250 g	500 g
Brown rice (uncooked)	125 g	250 g	500 g
Button mushrooms, halved	250 g	500 g	1 kg
Green sweet peppers, seeded and chopped	1	2	4
Salt	5 ml	10 ml	18 ml
Freshly ground black pepper	2 ml	4 ml	8 ml
Mustard powder	5 ml	10 ml	20 ml
Dry white wine	500 ml	1 litre	1,5 litres
Chicken stock	250 ml	500 ml	1 litre
Fresh cream (optional)	100 ml	150 ml	250 ml

Preparation

☐ Peel and cut the onions into rings.
☐ Cube the bacon.
☐ Halve the mushrooms.
☐ Seed and chop the sweet peppers.

Method

Brown the chicken portions in heated oil. Remove. Sauté the onions and bacon until the onions are translucent. Place the rice in an ovenproof dish and spoon the chicken and onion mixture on top. Sprinkle the mushrooms, sweet peppers and seasonings over. Pour the heated wine and stock, and the optional cream, over. Cover with the lid and bake for 2 hours at 180 °C (350 °F) or until the chicken is done. Add more liquid if necessary.

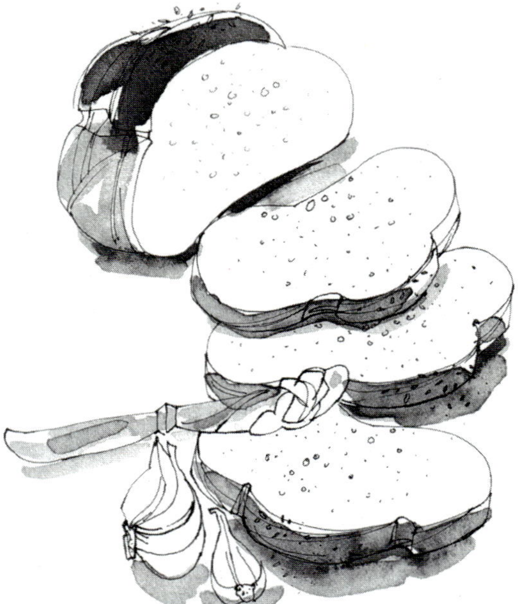

Baked chocolate custard

(12 servings; use 2 or 4 times the quantities for 24 or 48 servings and make in separate containers)

8 large eggs
2 ml salt
500 ml milk
500 ml fresh cream
60 ml sugar
10 ml vanilla essence
80 ml cocoa

Method

Beat the eggs, salt and milk together. Heat the milk mixture, cream and sugar to lukewarm. Add the vanilla essence and cocoa and pour the mixture into an ovenproof dish. Place in a pan of boiling water and bake for 45 minutes at 160 °C (325 °F) or until the egg custard has set.

Menu

Garlic bread/herb bread*

Chicken and rice casserole*
Buttered broccoli and cauliflower
Mixed salad with celery and apple

Baked chocolate custard*

For 12 people you will need:

☐ 1 bread (20 slices)
☐ 2 kg broccoli and cauliflower
☐ salad ingredients:
1 medium lettuce
4 medium red apples
3 celery stalks
100 ml mayonnaise
50 g chopped nuts

Curried fish

Ingredients	12 servings	24 servings	48 servings
Cooking oil	30 ml	45 ml	60 ml
Medium onions, cut into rings	300 g (3)	600 g (6)	1,2 kg (12)
Turmeric	10 ml	20 ml	40 ml
Mild curry powder	40 ml	75 ml	150 ml
Bay leaves	4	6	9
Brown vinegar	750 ml	1,25 litres	2 litres
Water	125 ml	250 ml	500 ml
Smooth apricot jam	80 ml	150 ml	250 ml
Salt	20 ml	40 ml	50 ml
Sugar	25 ml	50 ml	100 ml
White fish, e.g. hake, cut into portions	1,25 kg	2,5 kg	5 kg
Cake flour	15-20 ml	30-40 ml	65-70 ml

Preparation
- ☐ Peel and cut the onions into rings.
- ☐ Cut the fish into portions.

Method
Heat the oil, add the onions and sauté them until they are translucent. Add the turmeric and curry powder and fry for a few minutes. Add the bay leaves, vinegar, water, jam, salt and sugar and simmer for 20 minutes. Add the fish and simmer for 20-30 minutes or until the fish is done. Thicken the sauce, if necessary, with flour mixed to a paste with water.

Tip
☐ Don't add all the flour paste at once. First add half, cook until thickened and check the consistency. Add the rest, if necessary.

Spiced peaches

(12 servings; use 2 or 4 times the quantities for 24 or 48 servings, but 1½ or 3 times the quantity of vinegar)

2 cans (2 x 410 g) peach halves, drained and syrup reserved
50 ml grape vinegar
100 ml sugar
5 ml chopped fresh ginger
1 ml cloves
1 cinnamon stick

Method
Heat the peach canning syrup, vinegar, sugar and flavourings until the sugar has dissolved. Pour over the peaches and chill.

Menu

Curried fish*
Almond rice
Poppadums
Minted peas
Sweet pepper sambal*
Spiced peaches*

Fresh fruit platter

For 12 people you will need:
- ☐ 400 g rice
- ☐ 12 poppadums
- ☐ 1,1 kg frozen peas
- ☐ 4 each fresh fruit (guavas, nartjies, oranges, apples) – winter
- ☐ 4 each fresh fruit (peaches, apricots, mangoes, bananas) – summer

Fish in parsley batter

Ingredients	12 servings	24 servings	48 servings
White fish portions (about 150 g each)	12	24	48
Salt	25 ml	50 ml	100 ml
White pepper	3 ml	8 ml	15 ml
Cake flour	200 ml (100 g)	400 ml (200 g)	700 ml (350 g)
Cooking oil for deep-frying			
Parsley batter:			
Cake flour	2 x 250 ml (240 g)	4 x 250 ml (480 g)	8 x 250 ml (960 g)
Baking powder	10 ml	20 ml	40 ml
Salt	3 ml	5 ml	8 ml
Chopped fresh parsley	30 ml	50 ml	75 ml
Eggs	4	8	16
Water	400 ml	750 ml	1,25 litres

Preparation

☐ Cut the fish into portions.

☐ Prepare the parsley batter: Sift the dry ingredients together and add the parsley. Mix well. Beat the eggs and water together and add to the flour mixture. Mix to a smooth batter. Allow to rest in the refrigerator for 15 minutes.

Method

Pat the fish portions dry with paper towels and season with salt and pepper. Roll the fish in flour, covering completely. Dip each fish portion in parsley batter and deep-fry in oil until golden brown and cooked.

Tartar sauce

(12 servings; use 2 or 4 times the quantities for 24 or 48 servings)

250 ml mayonnaise
1 onion, finely chopped
6 gherkins, chopped
20 sweet pickles, chopped
4 ml prepared mustard
10 ml lemon juice

Method

Mix all the ingredients together thoroughly and chill.

Menu

Fish in parsley batter*
Tartar sauce*
Chips
Fried onion rings
Mixed green vegetables

Fresh fruit and cheese

For 12 people you will need:

☐ 1,8 kg potatoes
☐ 6 large onions
☐ 1,1 kg mixed green vegetables
☐ fruit:
12 apples
☐ cheese:
300 g Cheddar cheese
250 g brie

Chutney chicken

Ingredients	12 servings	24 servings	48 servings
Chicken portions (drumsticks, thighs or breasts)	12	24	48
Salt	10 ml	20 ml	30 ml
Freshly ground black pepper	3 ml	6 ml	10 ml
Cake flour	200 ml (100 g)	400 ml (200 g)	800 ml (400 g)
Cooking oil	100 ml	200 ml	400 ml
Chutney sauce:			
Fruit chutney	250 ml	500 ml	1 litre
Mayonnaise	250 ml	500 ml	1 litre
Boiling water	300 ml	600 ml	1 litre
Brown onion soup powder	2 packets	4 packets	8 packets

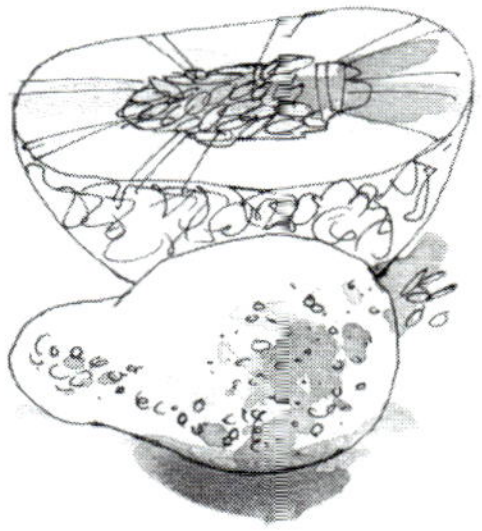

Preparation

☐ Mix the salt, pepper and flour.

Method

Prepare the chicken: Roll the chicken servings in flavoured flour and fry in heated oil in a heavy-based saucepan until golden brown. Arrange in a single layer in an ovenproof dish.

Prepare the chutney sauce: Mix all the ingredients thoroughly and pour over the chicken. Cover with aluminium foil and bake for 1 hour at 180 °C (350 °F). Turn at least once while cooking.

Remove the aluminium foil and bake the chicken, uncovered, for a further 10 minutes or until golden brown.

Menu

Fish soup*

Chutney chicken*
Brown rice
Braised green beans
Pumpkin slices with honeyed orange sauce*
Fresh green salad with avocado

Melon balls in port

For 12 people you will need:

☐ 400 g rice
☐ 1,2 kg green beans
☐ salad ingredients:
300 g young spinach leaves (tough stalks removed)
2 medium green sweet peppers
12 chives
3 medium avocados
☐ 3 medium melons
☐ 80 ml port

Food for friends

There's a saying that goes: "The more the merrier". Invite a few friends – or your entire social circle – for a party. On a balmy summer evening gather around the braai fire or, in winter, around a friendly fire in the fireplace. Here are recipes for one-dish meals that can be prepared in advance and give the hostess lots of time to socialise. There are also a few ideas for something interesting over the coals . . .

Above from left: Fresh fruit (menu, p. 37) and Lasagne (p. 37). Bottom left: Oxtail stew with red wine (p. 36), served with Flambé vegetables (p. 36). Front right: Green salad (menu, p. 36).

Oxtail stew with red wine

Ingredients	12 servings	24 servings	48 servings
Oxtail, cut at joints and trimmed of excess fat	3 x 1 kg	6 x 1 kg	12 x 1 kg
Cooking oil	20 ml	50 ml	100 ml
Medium onions, finely chopped	300 g (3)	500 g (5)	1 kg (10)
Garlic cloves, crushed	3	4	8
Salt	15 ml	30 ml	60 ml
Freshly ground black pepper	3 ml	5 ml	10 ml
Chopped fresh parsley	30 ml	60 ml	100 ml
Dried or chopped fresh thyme	5 ml or 15 ml	10 ml or 30 ml	20 ml or 60 ml
Dried or chopped fresh rosemary	5 ml or 15 ml	10 ml or 30 ml	20 ml or 60 ml
Bay leaves	3	6	12
Dry red wine	750 ml	1,5 litres	2,5 litres
Meat stock	750 ml	1,5 litres	2,5 litres
Cake flour	30 ml (15 g)	60 ml (30 g)	125 ml (60 g)

Preparation

☐ Prepare the meat.
☐ Peel and chop the onions.
☐ Peel and crush the garlic.
☐ Chop the herbs.

Method

Brown the meat in heated oil in a heavy-based saucepan. Add the chopped onions and crushed garlic and sauté until the onions are translucent.

Add the seasonings and heated red wine and stock. Cover with the lid, reduce the heat and simmer for 2½-3 hours or until the meat is tender. Thicken the gravy with the flour mixed to a paste with water.

Tip

☐ Add peeled new potatoes 45 minutes before the end of cooking (allow 1 potato per person).

Flambé vegetables

(48 servings; use ¼ or ½ of the quantities for 12 or 24 servings)

1,5 kg pickling onions
180 ml butter
180 ml cooking oil
360 g leeks, sliced
600 g baby carrots, blanched
1,2 kg brown mushrooms, sliced
200 g celery stalks, chopped
1,2 kg baby marrows, chopped
1,5 litres white meat stock
360 ml chopped fresh parsley
360 ml brandy

Method

Sauté the pickling onions in the heated butter and oil. Add the leeks, carrots, mushrooms, celery and baby marrows and fry for a few minutes. Add the stock and simmer for 10 minutes. Drain and add the parsley. Heat the brandy, flame and pour it over the vegetables. Serve immediately.

Menu

Cream of asparagus soup

Oxtail stew with red wine*
New potatoes
Flambé vegetables*
Green salad

Baked lemon pudding*

For 12 people you will need:

☐ 2,4 litres cream of asparagus soup
☐ 1,1 kg new potatoes
☐ salad ingredients:
1 medium lettuce
1 medium cucumber
125 ml chopped fresh herbs (parsley, dill, basil)
3 small avocados

Lasagne

Ingredients	12 servings	24 servings	48 servings
Minced topside	1 kg	2,3 kg	4,5 kg
Cooking oil	15 ml	30 ml	50 ml
Medium onions, finely chopped	200 g (2)	400 g (4)	800 g (8)
Garlic cloves, crushed	2	3	6
Tomatoes, skinned and coarsely chopped	300 g (3)	600 g (6)	1,2 kg (12)
Tomato paste	100 ml	200 ml	360 ml
Salt	7 ml	15 ml	30 ml
Freshly ground black pepper	2 ml	4 ml	8 ml
Brown sugar	15 ml	30 ml	60 ml
Dried or chopped fresh basil	3 ml or 10 ml	5 ml or 15 ml	15 ml or 45 ml
Meat stock	300 ml	600 ml	1,2 litres
Chopped fresh parsley	50 ml	100 ml	200 ml
Parmesan cheese	30 g	60 g	120 g
Béchamel sauce:			
Milk	1,2 litres	2,4 litres	4,8 litres
Carrots	100 g (1)	200 g (2)	400 g (4)
Celery stalks	50 g (2)	100 g (4)	200 g (8)
Black peppercorns	5	10	20
Mace	1 ml	2 ml	4 ml
Butter	100 g	220 g	450 g
Cake flour	100 ml (50 g)	225 ml (110 g)	450 ml (220 g)
Salt	2 ml	5 ml	10 ml
Lasagne noodles:			
Lasagne noodles	300 g	600 g	1,2 kg

Preparation

☐ Peel and chop the onions.
☐ Peel and crush the garlic cloves.
☐ Skin and chop the tomatoes.
☐ Chop the herbs.
☐ Prepare the flavoured milk by heating the milk with the carrots, celery stalks, black peppercorns and mace and then straining it. Allow to cool.

Method

Fry the mince in heated oil in a heavy-based saucepan until it changes colour. Add the onions and garlic and sauté until the onions are translucent. Add the tomatoes, tomato paste, seasonings, sugar, basil and heated stock. Reduce the heat, cover with the lid and simmer for 1 hour. Add the parsley.

Prepare the béchamel sauce: Melt the butter in a saucepan and stir in the flour. Add the flavoured milk, a little at a time, to make a smooth mixture. Season with salt. Heat over low heat, stirring constantly. Cook until thickened.

Layer the noodles, meat mixture and béchamel sauce alternately into an ovenproof dish. Repeat the layers two to three times, and end with béchamel sauce. Sprinkle Parmesan cheese over and bake in a preheated oven at 180 °C (350 °F) until golden brown.

Menu

Tomato and mozzarella salad with fresh basil*

Lasagne*
Fresh green salad with Greek dressing*
Olive bread* with anchovy butter

Fresh fruit
Cheese and biscuits

For 12 people you will need:

☐ salad ingredients:
1 medium lettuce
250 g broccoli
1 large green sweet pepper
4 medium baby marrows
☐ 60 g anchovy butter
☐ fruit:
1,8 kg melon and/or watermelon balls
☐ cheese:
250 g herbed cottage cheese
250 g Gouda cheese
☐ 36 (3 kinds x 12 each) savoury biscuits

Paprika beef

Ingredients	12 servings	24 servings	48 servings
Thick rib of beef, cut into 20 mm thick slices	1,5 kg	3 kg	6 kg
Cooking oil	40 ml	70 ml	150 ml
Medium onions, chopped	100 g (1)	200 g (2)	400 g (4)
Meat stock	350 ml	750 ml	1,5 litres
Salt	10 ml	15 ml	30 ml
Freshly ground black pepper	3 ml	5 ml	10 ml
Paprika	8 ml	15 ml	30 ml
Large tomatoes, chopped	200 g (2)	300 g (3)	600 g (6)
Tomato paste	1 x 65 g	2 x 65 g	3 x 65 g
Green sweet peppers, seeded and cut into julienne strips	2	4	7
Cake flour	20 ml (10 g)	40 ml (20 g)	60 ml (30 g)
Sour cream	200 ml	400 ml	800 ml

Preparation

☐ Slice the meat.
☐ Peel and chop the onions.
☐ Skin and chop the tomatoes.
☐ Seed the green sweet peppers and cut them into julienne strips.

Method

Brown the meat in heated oil in a heavy-based saucepan. Add the onions and sauté until translucent. Add the heated stock, seasonings, tomatoes and tomato paste. Cover with the lid, reduce the heat and simmer for 1½-2 hours or until the meat is tender. Add the sweet peppers and simmer for a further 15 minutes. Thicken the sauce with the flour mixed to a paste with water. Remove from the stove and add the sour cream.

Tip

☐ This dish also freezes very successfully for up to a month. Add the sweet peppers and sour cream when the dish is reheated.

Baked mushrooms

(12 servings; use 2 or 4 times the quantities for 24 or 48 servings)

12 large brown mushrooms
120 ml fresh breadcrumbs
120 ml grated Cheddar cheese
60 ml Parmesan cheese
5 ml cayenne pepper
50 ml butter

Method

Place the mushrooms in an ovenproof dish. Mix the breadcrumbs and Cheddar cheese and sprinkle over the mushrooms. Sprinkle the Parmesan cheese and cayenne pepper over. Dot with butter. Bake for 20 minutes in a preheated oven at 180 °C (350 °F).

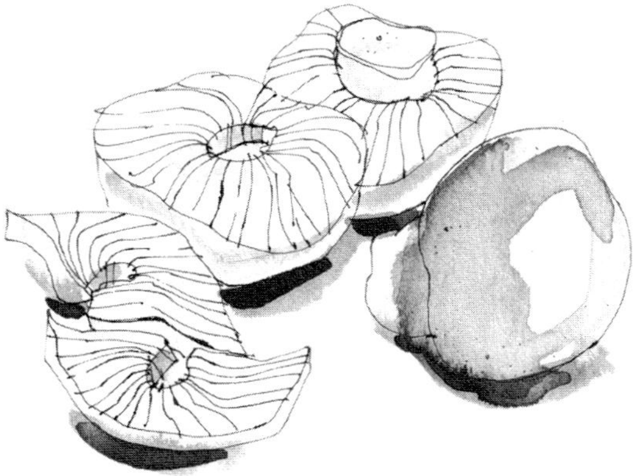

Menu

Baked mushrooms*

Paprika beef*
Couscous or rice
Green beans with baby onions
Butternut with cinnamon
French salad

Vanilla ice cream with chopped nuts

For 12 people you will need:

☐ 400 g couscous or rice
☐ 1,2 kg green beans
☐ 6 medium butternuts
☐ salad ingredients:
1 medium lettuce
1 medium cucumber
4 medium carrots
4 medium tomatoes
1 medium onion
☐ 1,2 litres ice cream
☐ 240 g nuts (walnuts, pecan nuts or almonds)

Tomato bredie

Ingredients	**12 servings**	**24 servings**	**48 servings**
Boned thick rib of lamb, cut into 20 mm cubes	1 kg	1,8 kg	3,6 kg
Breast of lamb, sawn into 30 mm portions	1 kg	1,8 kg	3,6 kg
Cooking oil	20 ml	35 ml	70 ml
Medium onions, chopped	300 g (3)	600 g (6)	1,2 kg (12)
Garlic cloves, crushed	2	4	7
Salt	10 ml	20 ml	60 ml
Freshly ground black pepper	3 ml	6 ml	12 ml
Dried or chopped fresh basil	3 ml or 10 ml	5 ml or 15 ml	15 ml or 45 ml
Canned tomatoes, chopped	1 x 410 g	3 x 410 g	5 x 410 g
Tomato purée	40 ml	80 ml	150 ml
White peppercorns	6	12	24
Sugar	8 ml	15 ml	30 ml
Potatoes, quartered	600 g (4)	1,2 kg (8)	2,5 kg (15)

Preparation
☐ Prepare the meat.
☐ Peel and chop the onions.
☐ Peel and crush the garlic cloves.
☐ Chop the tomatoes and reserve the liquid.
☐ Peel and quarter the potatoes.

Method
Brown the meat in heated oil in a heavy-based saucepan. Add the onions and garlic and sauté until the onions are translucent. Add the seasonings, tomatoes and liquid, tomato purée, peppercorns and sugar. Reduce the heat, cover with the lid and simmer for 1½ hours. Add the potatoes and simmer for a further 45 minutes or until the potatoes are cooked.

Tips
☐ If the lamb has a lot of visible fat, use less cooking oil.
☐ Freshly chopped basil or a basil sprig can be used for garnishing.
☐ Three large ripe tomatoes can be used instead of one can of tomatoes.

Smoked snoek pâté

(48 servings; use ¼ or ½ of the quantities for 12 or 24 servings)

800 g smoked snoek, flaked
750 ml smooth cottage cheese
6 medium onions, finely chopped
25 ml mixed dried herbs
25 ml paprika
12,5 ml salt
8 ml white pepper
40 ml parsley, finely chopped

Method
Place the snoek, cottage cheese, onions, herbs and seasonings in a food processor and process to a creamy mixture. Spoon into serving dishes and sprinkle parsley over. Serve with fresh whole-wheat bread.

Menu

Fresh whole-wheat bread with smoked snoek pâté*

Tomato bredie*
Pearl wheat
Braised green beans
Pumpkin fritters
Fresh green salad

Apple tart with cream

For 12 people you will need:
☐ 1 whole-wheat loaf (20 slices)
☐ 500 ml pearl wheat
☐ 1,2 kg green beans
☐ 1,2 litres cooked pumpkin
☐ salad ingredients:
200 g butter lettuce
150 g watercress
8 chives
6 medium baby marrows
150 g lucerne sprouts
☐ 2 apple tarts, each 225 mm in diameter (12 servings of 150 g each)
☐ 240 ml cream

Chicken stir-fry

Ingredients	12 servings	24 servings	48 servings
Chicken breasts, boned, skinned and cut into strips	12	24	48
Cooking oil	40 ml	75 ml	120 ml
Medium onions, cut into rings	300 g (3)	600 g (6)	1,2 kg (12)
Red sweet peppers, seeded and cut into julienne strips	3	6	12
Green sweet peppers, seeded and cut into julienne strips	3	6	12
Carrots, cut into julienne strips	400 g (4)	700 g (7)	1,2 kg (12)
Button mushrooms, halved	250 g	400 g	700 g
Chopped fresh parsley	10 ml	15 ml	25 ml
Salt	7 ml	15 ml	25 ml
Freshly ground black pepper	1 ml	2 ml	3 ml
Sweet-and-sour sauce (commercial)	200 ml	350 ml	650 ml

Above left: Greek salad with feta cheese (menu, p. 42). Above centre: Brown mushrooms with garlic (p. 42). Above right: Sliced biltong (menu, p. 42) is served with whole-wheat bread (bottom left). Front right: Chicken sosaties (p. 42), served with Boerewors spirals (menu, p. 42).

Preparation

☐ Bone, skin and cut the chicken breasts into strips.
☐ Peel and prepare the vegetables.
☐ Chop the parsley.

Method

Fry the chicken in heated oil. Add the onions and sauté until translucent. Add the sweet peppers, carrots and mushrooms and stir-fry lightly. Sprinkle the parsley and seasonings over, add the sweet-and-sour sauce and simmer for 3 minutes. Serve immediately.

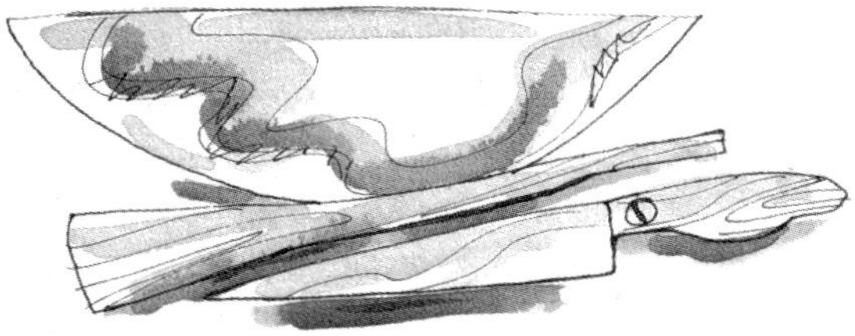

Chocolate fondue with marshmallows

(12 servings; use 2 or 4 times the quantities for 24 or 48 servings)

600 g cooking chocolate
12 marshmallows
300 ml cream
3 ml vanilla essence or brandy

Method

Melt the chocolate in a double boiler and add the marshmallows. Add the cream and vanilla essence and mix until smooth. Use as a dip for sponge fingers, fresh fruit cut into portions and marshmallows.

Menu

Chicken stir-fry*
Shell noodles or white rice
Selection of skewered fruit
Fresh whole-wheat bread and butter

Chocolate fondue with marshmallows*

For 12 people you will need:

☐ 500 g shell noodles or 400 g rice: serve cooked shell noodles immediately.
☐ fruit:
1 medium pineapple
3 large mangoes
4 medium kiwi fruit
12 large strawberries
24 bamboo skewers
☐ 1 whole-wheat loaf (20 slices)
☐ 60 g butter

Chicken sosaties

Ingredients	12 servings	24 servings	48 servings
Chicken breasts, boned, skinned and cut into 25 mm cubes	12	24	48
Pickling onions, halved (optional)	24	48	96
Bamboo skewers	24	48	96
Curry marinade:			
Large onions, cut into rings	300 g (2)	600 g (4)	1,2 kg (8)
Cooking oil	30 ml	50 ml	80 ml
Mild curry powder	30 ml	60 ml	100 ml
Turmeric	5 ml	10 ml	17 ml
Boiling water	500 ml	800 ml	1,5 litres
Smooth apricot jam	150 ml	250 ml	400 ml
Brown wine vinegar	500 ml	750 ml	1,2 litres
Brown sugar	30 ml	50 ml	75 ml

Preparation

☐ Bone, skin and cube the chicken breasts.
☐ Halve the pickling onions.
☐ Soak the bamboo skewers in water.
☐ Prepare the marinade by sautéing the onions in heated oil until translucent. Add the curry powder and turmeric and fry for 2 minutes. Add the boiling water, jam, vinegar and sugar and mix well. Simmer for 10 minutes and allow to cool.

Method

Thread the chicken and pickling onions alternately onto the bamboo skewers and pack them into a plastic or ceramic container. Pour the marinade over and marinate overnight in a cool place. Drain the sosaties and braai them over moderate coals or 100 mm below the oven grilling element.

Brown mushrooms with garlic

(12 servings; use 2 or 4 times the quantities for 24 or 48 servings)

12 large brown mushrooms
6 garlic cloves, chopped
10 ml lemon juice
salt and freshly ground black pepper to taste
35 ml butter

Method

Wipe the mushrooms with paper towels. Sprinkle the garlic, lemon juice, salt and pepper over and dot with butter. Bake for about 20-30 minutes at 180 °C (350 °F) or until cooked.

Menu

Sliced biltong and whole-wheat bread

Chicken sosaties*
Boerewors spirals
Jacket potatoes with sour cream
Brown mushrooms with garlic*
Greek salad with feta cheese

Fruit salad with ice cream

For 12 people you will need:

☐ 300 g beef biltong
☐ 1 whole-wheat loaf (20 slices)
☐ 1,2 kg lamb sausage
☐ 12 bamboo skewers

Soak the bamboo skewers in water for 30 minutes. Cut the sausage into 20 cm lengths and roll them up to form spirals. Insert a skewer through each spiral.

☐ 2,4 kg potatoes
☐ 500 ml sour cream
☐ salad ingredients:
1 medium lettuce
1 medium cucumber
3 medium tomatoes
1 small onion
250 g feta cheese
24 olives
☐ fruit salad:
1 large pawpaw
3 medium bananas
1 small pineapple
200 g strawberries
8 granadillas
☐ 1,2 litres ice cream

Fish and vegetable parcels

Ingredients	12 servings	24 servings	48 servings
Fish fillets (about 150 g each)	12	24	48
Butter, melted	100 g	200 g	350 g
Lemon juice	25 ml	50 ml	100 ml
Chives, chopped	60 ml	120 ml	250 ml
Carrots, cut into julienne strips	400 g (4)	800 g (8)	1,6 kg (16)
Baby marrows, thinly sliced	5	10	20
Button mushrooms, sliced	200 g	350 g	600 g
Salt	15 ml	30 ml	60 ml
Freshly ground black pepper	5 ml	10 ml	20 ml
Chopped fresh parsley	60 ml	120 ml	250 ml

Preparation

☐ Tear aluminium foil into squares large enough for each parcel.
☐ Prepare the vegetables.
☐ Chop the parsley.

Method

Place each fish fillet on an aluminium foil square. Sprinkle melted butter and lemon juice over. Place a little of each kind of vegetable on the fish fillet and season with salt and pepper. Sprinkle parsley over and close the parcel securely. Bake for 45 minutes in a preheated oven at 180 °C (350 °F) or until the fish and vegetables are cooked.

Tip

☐ The parcels can also be cooked over moderate coals.

Mouthwatering baked potatoes

(12 servings; use 2 or 4 times the quantities for 24 or 48 servings)

12 medium potatoes, washed
100 ml melted butter
1 packet brown onion soup powder

Method

Make evenly spaced incisions in the potatoes. Pack the potatoes in a shallow ovenproof dish. Mix the butter and onion soup and pour over the potatoes. Cover and bake the potatoes for 1 hour at 180 °C (350 °F) or until cooked.

Menu

Grilled rib of pork

Fish and vegetable parcels*
Mouthwatering baked potatoes*
Oven-baked pickling onions*
Tomato and onion salad with fresh herbs

Fruit salad

For 12 people you will need:

☐ 1,5 kg grilled rib of pork
☐ salad ingredients:
6 large tomatoes
3 medium onions
125 ml chopped fresh herbs
☐ fruit salad:
2 melons
½ watermelon
4 medium kiwi fruit

Hassle-free get-togethers

For an informal get-together, it's important to choose dishes that need little last-minute preparation and won't cost a fortune. Although most of the ingredients in these recipes are ones you'll have available, each dish is transformed into a taste sensation with the addition of one or two special ingredients ...

Above centre: Caramel banana dessert (p. 48). Front right: Buttered young onions and green beans (menu, p. 48). Front left: Beef stroganoff (p. 48).

Steak and kidney pie

Ingredients	12 servings	24 servings	48 servings
Boned thick rib of beef, cut into 20 mm cubes	1,5 kg	3 kg	6 kg
Lambs' kidneys, cut into 20 mm cubes	500 g	1 kg	2 kg
Cooking oil	50 ml	100 ml	200 ml
Medium onions, chopped	200 g (2)	400 g (4)	800 g (8)
Garlic cloves, crushed	3	6	12
Salt	10 ml	20 ml	40 ml
Freshly ground black pepper	3 ml	5 ml	10 ml
Bay leaves	2	4	8
Worcester sauce	30 ml	50 ml	100 ml
Meat stock	500 ml	1 litre	2 litres
Cake flour	50 ml (25 g)	100 ml (50 g)	200 ml (100 g)
Parsley, chopped	75 ml	150 ml	250 ml
Topping:			
Milk	250 ml	500 ml	1 litre
Cooking oil	250 ml	500 ml	1 litre
Eggs	2	4	8
Cake flour	2 x 250 ml (240 g)	4 x 250 ml (480 g)	8 x 250 ml (1 kg)
Baking powder	20 ml	40 ml	80 ml
Salt	4 ml	8 ml	16 ml

Preparation

☐ Cube the meat.
☐ Remove the cores and membranes from the kidneys and cube.
☐ Peel and chop the onions.
☐ Peel and crush the garlic cloves.
☐ Chop the parsley.

Method

Brown the meat and kidneys in heated oil in a heavy-based saucepan. Add the onions and garlic and sauté until the onions are translucent. Add the seasonings, Worcester sauce and heated stock. Reduce heat, cover, and simmer for 1½-2 hours or until the meat is tender. Thicken the gravy with flour mixed to a paste with water. Add parsley and mix.

Prepare the topping: Beat the milk, oil and eggs together. Sift the dry ingredients and add the milk mixture. Mix to make a runny batter.

Spoon meat into an ovenproof dish. Allow to cool slightly and pour topping over. Bake 20 minutes in a preheated oven at 180 °C (350 °F) or until golden brown and cooked.

Layered mixed salad

(12 servings; use 2 or 4 times the quantities for 24 or 48 servings)

6 ripe tomatoes, sliced
1 large green sweet pepper, cut into strips
¾ English cucumber, cut into strips
2 small onions, cut into rings
250 g mozzarella cheese, sliced
15 black olives
basil for garnishing

Dressing
150 ml salad oil
100 ml white wine vinegar
50 ml mayonnaise
5 ml mustard powder
salt and black pepper to taste
25 ml sugar
20 ml dried or 60 ml chopped fresh mixed herbs

Method

Prepare the salad by layering all the ingredients in a glass salad bowl in the order in which

Menu

Steak and kidney pie*
Wild rice
Buttered green vegetables
Layered mixed salad*

Stewed dried fruit with custard

For 12 people you will need:
☐ 400 g wild rice
☐ 1,1 kg mixed green vegetables
☐ 300 g dried fruit (unsoaked)
☐ 600 ml custard

they are given. Prepare the salad dressing by mixing all the ingredients together thoroughly. Pour the dressing over the salad just before serving and garnish it with basil.

Tips

☐ Prepare the salad dressing a few hours in advance to give the flavours time to develop.
☐ Feta cheese may be used instead of the mozzarella.

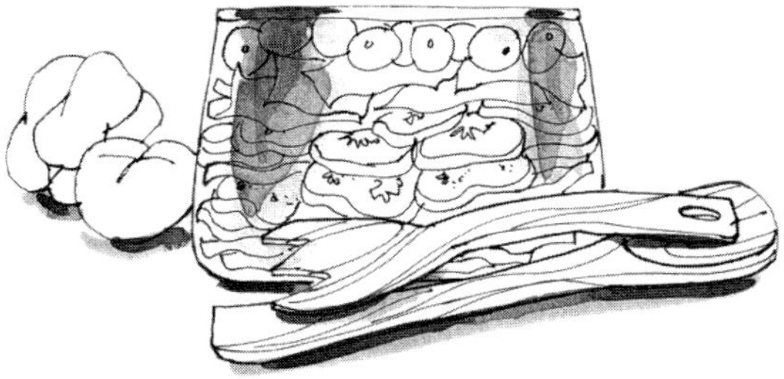

Menu

Smoked snoek pâté* with whole-wheat bread

Burgundy beef*
Pearl wheat
Green salad with croutons*

Easy ice cream* with caramel sauce*

For 12 people you will need:
☐ 1 whole-wheat loaf (20 slices)
☐ 500 ml pearl wheat
☐ salad ingredients:
1 medium lettuce
200 g bean sprouts
3 medium avocados
6 spring onions

Burgundy beef

Ingredients	12 servings	24 servings	48 servings
Boned thick rib of beef, cut into 20 mm thick slices	1,3 kg	2,6 kg	5 kg
Pickled pork, cut into 20 mm cubes	250 g	500 g	1 kg
Cooking oil	30 ml	60 ml	100 ml
Meat stock	700 ml	1,2 litres	2 litres
Dry red wine	500 ml	1 litre	2 litres
Salt	10 ml	20 ml	40 ml
Freshly ground black pepper	5 ml	10 ml	15 ml
Dried or chopped fresh thyme	5 ml or 15 ml	15 ml or 45 ml	30 ml or 100 ml
Carrots, sliced	400 g (4)	800 g (8)	1,5 kg (15)
Mushrooms, sliced	600 g	1,5 kg	2,5 kg
Cake flour	50 ml (25 g)	100 ml (50 g)	200 ml (100 g)
Whole pickling onions	500 g	1,2 kg	2 kg
Butter	45 g	100 g	150 g
Chopped fresh parsley	100 ml	200 ml	400 ml

Preparation

☐ Prepare the meat.
☐ Peel and slice the carrots.
☐ Slice the mushrooms.
☐ Peel the pickling onions.
☐ Chop the parsley.

Method

Brown the meat in heated oil in a heavy-based saucepan. Add the heated stock and wine. Add the salt, pepper and thyme. Cover with the lid, reduce the heat and simmer for 1-1½ hours or until the meat is almost tender. Add the carrots and mushrooms and simmer for a further 30 minutes or until the vegetables are tender. Thicken the gravy with the flour mixed to a paste with water. Sauté onions in heated butter until tender and translucent. Spoon on top of dish and garnish with parsley.

Easy ice cream

(12 servings; use 2 or 4 times the quantities for 24 or 48 servings)

250 ml cream
1 can (410 g) evaporated milk (refrigerated overnight)
1 can (397 g) condensed milk
3 ml vanilla essence

Method

Beat the cream and evaporated milk separately until stiff. Fold the condensed milk into the evaporated milk, as well as the cream and vanilla essence. Freeze until firm in a flat container.

Beef stroganoff

Ingredients	12 servings	24 servings	48 servings
Bolo or thick rib, cut into 5 mm strips	2 kg	4 kg	8 kg
Cooking oil	25 ml	50 ml	100 ml
Medium onions, chopped	500 g (5)	1 kg (10)	2 kg (20)
Garlic cloves, crushed	3	6	12
Salt	10 ml	20 ml	40 ml
Freshly ground black pepper	3 ml	5 ml	10 ml
Meat stock	250 ml	500 ml	1 litre
Dry white wine	200 ml	400 ml	800 ml
Lemon juice	20 ml	40 ml	80 ml
Mushrooms, chopped	1 kg	2 kg	4 kg
Cake flour	30 ml (15 g)	60 ml (30 g)	125 ml (60 g)
Sour cream	250 ml	500 ml	750 ml
Milk	250 ml	500 ml	750 ml
Chopped fresh parsley	50 ml	100 ml	200 ml

Preparation

- ☐ Cut the meat into strips.
- ☐ Peel and chop the onions.
- ☐ Peel and crush the garlic cloves.
- ☐ Chop the mushrooms.
- ☐ Chop the parsley.

Method

Brown the meat in heated oil in a heavy-based saucepan. Add the onions and garlic and sauté until the onions are translucent. Add the seasonings, heated stock, wine and lemon juice. Reduce the heat, cover with the lid and simmer for 1 hour or until the meat is almost tender. Add the mushrooms and simmer for a further 30 minutes. Thicken the sauce with the flour mixed to a paste with water.

Mix the sour cream and milk and pour the mixture over the meat. Garnish with chopped parsley.

Caramel banana dessert

(12 servings; use 2 or 4 times the quantities for 24 or 48 servings)

1 flan case
50 ml brandy
1 can (225 g) caramel condensed milk
3 bananas, sliced
20 ml lemon juice
200 ml cream
cocoa and fresh mint for garnish

Method

Place flan case on a cake plate and sprinkle brandy over. Spread condensed milk over and arrange banana slices on top. Sprinkle lemon juice over to prevent discoloration. Beat cream until stiff and pipe it over, using a piping bag. Sprinkle cocoa over and garnish.

Rice timbales

(12 servings; use 2 or 4 times the quantities for 24 or 48 servings)

1,5 litres hot cooked rice (500 g uncooked rice)
60 ml melted butter
25 ml chopped fresh herbs

Method

Mix all the ingredients thoroughly and press them firmly into greased cups. Allow to cool slightly and turn out onto a serving dish.

Variation

Parsley rice timbales: Use 2 ml chopped parsley instead of 2 ml fresh herbs.

Menu

Fresh green salad with croutons*

Beef stroganoff*
Rice timbales*
Buttered young onions and green beans
Grilled pumpkin

Caramel banana dessert*

For 12 people you will need:

- ☐ salad ingredients:
  - *1 medium butter lettuce*
  - *125 ml chopped fresh herbs*
  - *6 radishes*
  - *100 g mangetout (optional)*
  - *¼ English cucumber*
- ☐ 18 young onions
- ☐ 1,2 kg green beans
- ☐ 2 kg pumpkin slices

Pickled tongue

Ingredients	12 servings	24 servings	48 servings
Pickled ox tongue	2 x 1 kg	4 x 1 kg	8 x 1 kg
Black peppercorns	10	20	40
Cloves, whole	2	3	5
Bay leaves	3	5	10
Medium onions, quartered	200 g (2)	300 g (3)	600 g (6)
Carrots, halved	100 g (1)	200 g (2)	400 g (4)

Preparation

- ☐ Peel and quarter the onions.
- ☐ Peel and halve the carrots.

Method

Place the tongues in a large saucepan and cover with cold water. Tie the peppercorns, cloves and bay leaves in a muslin bag and add to the tongues with the remaining ingredients. Heat to boiling point. Reduce the heat, cover with the lid and simmer for 3-4 hours or until the tongues are tender. Remove tongues from saucepan, immerse them in cold water to make handling easier and pull off the skins while still warm. Cool the tongues and slice thinly.

Fruit sauce

(48 servings; use ¼ or ½ of the quantities for 12 or 24 servings)

2 cans (2 x 810 g) apricots, sliced
350 ml brown sugar
8 ml mustard powder
400 g sultanas, soaked overnight
350 ml white grape vinegar
40 ml cornflour

Method

Place all the ingredients, except the cornflour, in a saucepan and heat to boiling point. Simmer until the sugar has dissolved. Thicken the sauce with the cornflour mixed to a paste with water. Cool and serve with the pickled tongue.

Home-made mayonnaise

(24 servings; use ½ or 2 times the quantities for 12 or 48 servings)

2 egg yolks
salt and pepper to taste
15 ml lemon juice
375 ml cooking oil
3 ml mustard powder

Method

Beat the egg yolks, salt, pepper and lemon juice in a small dish until thickened. Add the oil carefully, otherwise the mayonnaise will separate. Add the first 30 ml oil a drop at a time, beating constantly. The rest can be added slightly faster: 15 ml at a time in a thin stream, beating constantly. Season with mustard.

Tip

☐ Thin mayonnaise with 15 ml warm water if it's too thick. Important: All ingredients must be at room temperature.

Menu

Sun-dried tomatoes with whole-wheat bread

Pickled tongue* with fruit sauce*
Crushed wheat salad* with home-made mayonnaise*
Marinated broccoli and red sweet peppers*
Spring salad with fresh herbs

Meringue nests with strawberries and cream

For 12 people you will need:

- ☐ 500 g sun-dried tomatoes
- ☐ 1 whole-wheat loaf (20 slices)
- ☐ salad ingredients:
  1 medium butter lettuce
  peel and segments of 4 oranges, for garnish
  2 grapefruit
  125 ml chopped fresh herbs
- ☐ 12 meringue nests
- ☐ 700 g strawberries
- ☐ 250 ml cream

Frikkadels

Ingredients	12 servings	24 servings	48 servings
Minced pork	1 kg	2 kg	4 kg
Minced beef	1 kg	2 kg	4 kg
Medium onions, finely chopped	200 g (2)	500 g (5)	1 kg (10)
Fresh breadcrumbs	250 ml	500 ml	1 kg
Dried or chopped fresh thyme	5 ml or 15 ml	15 ml or 45 ml	30 ml or 100 ml
Salt	15 ml	30 ml	60 ml
Freshly ground black pepper	3 ml	6 ml	12 ml

Menu

Cream of tomato soup with whole-wheat bread

Frikkadels* with savoury mushroom sauce*
Mashed potatoes
Buttered mixed vegetables
Green salad with bean sprouts

Ice cream with caramel sauce*

For 12 people you will need:
- ☐ 2,4 litres cream of tomato soup
- ☐ 1 whole-wheat loaf (20 slices)
- ☐ 1,8 kg potatoes
- ☐ 1,1 kg mixed vegetables
- ☐ salad ingredients:
  - *1 medium lettuce*
  - *2 medium green sweet peppers*
  - *6 spring onions*
  - *3 medium green apples*
  - *200 g bean sprouts*
- ☐ 1,2 litres ice cream

Preparation
- ☐ Peel and chop the onions finely.

Method
Place all the ingredients in a large mixing bowl and mix them lightly with two forks. Shape into 80 g frikkadels and arrange on a baking sheet. Bake for 30-45 minutes in a preheated oven at 160 °C (325 °F) or until cooked.

Savoury mushroom sauce

(12 servings; use 2 or 4 times the quantities for 24 or 48 servings)

500 g brown mushrooms, sliced
150 ml butter or margarine
80 ml (40 g) cake flour
750 ml milk
7 ml French mustard
3 ml salt
2 ml cayenne pepper

Method
Fry the mushrooms in butter until tender. Add the flour and mix thoroughly. Add the milk and stir over low heat until the sauce thickens. Season with mustard, salt and pepper.

Above left: Chicken with fruit chutney (p. 55). Above right: Buttered mixed vegetables (menu). Front left: Ratatouille with sweet peppers (p. 90). Bottom right: Frikkadels with savoury mushroom sauce.

Moussaka

Ingredients	12 servings	24 servings	48 servings
Minced topside	1,5 kg	3 kg	6 kg
Cooking oil	30 ml	60 ml	120 ml
Medium onions, finely chopped	300 g (3)	600 g (6)	1,2 kg (12)
Garlic cloves, crushed	4	8	16
Red wine	200 ml	400 ml	800 ml
Bay leaves	2	4	8
Dried or chopped fresh basil	5 ml or 15 ml	10 ml or 30 ml	20 ml or 60 ml
Chopped fresh parsley	75 ml	150 ml	300 ml
Tomato paste	80 ml	150 ml	300 ml
Canned tomatoes, chopped	2 x 410 g	4 x 410 g	8 x 410 g
Cayenne pepper	2 ml	3 ml	5 ml
Salt	7 ml	15 ml	30 ml
Freshly ground black pepper	3 ml	7 ml	15 ml
Sugar	10 ml	20 ml	30 ml
Medium brinjals, cut into 3 mm thick slices	3	6	12
Parmesan cheese	25 g	45 g	90 g
Béchamel sauce:			
Milk	750 ml	1,5 litres	3 litres
Onion, coarsely grated	100 g (1)	100 g (1)	200 g (2)
Black peppercorns	3	7	15
Bay leaves	3	5	10
Carrots, chopped	100 g (1)	200 g (2)	300 g (3)
Butter	80 g	160 g	320 g
Cake flour	80 ml (40 g)	150 ml (75 g)	300 ml (150 g)
Salt	3 ml	6 ml	12 ml
White pepper	0,5 ml	1 ml	2 ml

Preparation

☐ Peel and chop the onions finely.
☐ Peel and crush the garlic cloves.
☐ Chop the parsley.
☐ Chop the tomatoes.
☐ Slice the brinjals, sprinkle them with salt and set them aside for 30 minutes.
☐ Boil the milk, onion, peppercorns, bay leaves and carrots for 10 minutes over low heat. Pour the flavoured milk through a sieve and set aside.

Method

Fry the meat in heated oil in a heavy-based saucepan until changing colour. Add the onions and garlic and sauté until the onions are translucent. Add the heated wine, the bay leaves, basil, parsley, tomato paste, tomatoes, seasonings and sugar. Reduce the heat, cover with the lid and simmer for 45 minutes until done.

Prepare the béchamel sauce: Heat the flavoured milk. Melt the butter and add the flour and seasonings. Stir thoroughly to make a roux. Add the roux to the milk, stirring constantly. Heat to boiling point and simmer until the sauce thickens.

Rinse the brinjals under cold running water. Blanch the brinjals. Layer the meat mixture, béchamel sauce and brinjals alternately in an ovenproof dish, ending with a layer of béchamel sauce. Sprinkle Parmesan cheese over and bake for 20 minutes in a preheated oven at 180 °C (350 °F) or until golden brown.

Menu

Phyllo parcels with spinach*

Moussaka*
Garlic potbread*
Greek salad

Yoghurt with bananas*

For 12 people you will need:

☐ salad ingredients:
1 medium lettuce
1 medium cucumber
3 medium tomatoes
1 small onion
250 g feta cheese
24 olives

Crustless ham and cheese savoury tart

Ingredients	12 servings	24 servings	48 servings
Ham, chopped	400 g	750 g	1,5 kg
Eggs, beaten	6	12	24
Milk	750 ml	1,5 litres	3 litres
Cake flour	150 ml	300 ml	600 ml
Onion flakes	20 ml	25 ml	50 ml
Mustard powder	7,5 ml	15 ml	30 ml
Salt	3 ml	5 ml	8 ml
Lemon pepper	2 ml	3 ml	5 ml
Parsley, chopped	20 ml	40 ml	70 ml
Cheddar cheese, grated	400 g	750 g	1,5 kg

Preparation

- ☐ Chop the ham.
- ☐ Beat the eggs.
- ☐ Chop the parsley.
- ☐ Grate the cheese.

Method

Sprinkle the ham into the base of an ovenproof pie dish. Mix the beaten eggs and milk and add the flour, onion flakes and seasonings. Add the parsley and pour the egg mixture over the ham. Sprinkle the cheese over and bake for 40-50 minutes at 180 °C (350 °F) or until the egg mixture has set.

Tip

☐ If desired, the egg mixture can be poured into a cheese pastry case.

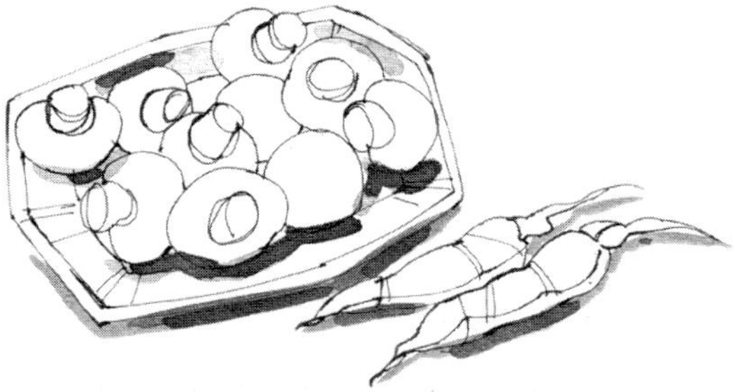

Cheese pastry for ham and cheese savoury tart

(12 servings; use 2 or 4 times the quantities for 24 or 48 servings)

375 ml (180 g) cake flour
180 ml grated Cheddar cheese
200 ml softened butter

Method

Mix all the ingredients to make a stiff dough. Line the pie dish with this pastry and pour the egg mixture into the uncooked crust. Bake as described.

Marinated mushrooms

(12 servings; use 2 or 4 times the quantities for 24 or 48 servings)

750 g button mushrooms, halved

Marinade

100 ml white meat stock
100 ml white wine
2 garlic cloves, crushed
30 ml olive oil
salt and freshly ground black pepper to taste
2 chillies, finely chopped
10 ml dried or 30 ml chopped fresh parsley
10 ml sugar

Method

Mix all the marinade ingredients and leave overnight for the flavour to develop. Pour over the mushrooms and marinate for 2-4 hours. Drain the mushrooms and serve chilled.

Menu

Crustless ham and cheese savoury tart*
Whole-wheat bread with herb butter
Marinated mushrooms*
Fresh green salad

Lemon sorbet with mango purée

For 12 people you will need:

- ☐ 1 whole-wheat loaf (20 slices)
- ☐ 60 g herb butter
- ☐ salad ingredients:
  - *1 medium lettuce*
  - *250 g broccoli*
  - *200 g cauliflower*
  - *1 large green sweet pepper*
- ☐ 1,2 litres lemon sorbet
- ☐ 3 large mangoes (for mango purée)

Savoury chicken

Ingredients	12 servings	24 servings	48 servings
Chicken portions (drumsticks, thighs or breasts)	12	24	48
Melted butter or cooking oil	30 ml	50 ml	80 ml
Bacon-flavoured biscuits, crushed	100 g	200 g	350 g
Parmesan cheese	40 g	75 g	130 g
Salt	5 ml	10 ml	20 ml
Cayenne pepper	3 ml	5 ml	8 ml
Freshly ground black pepper	3 ml	5 ml	8 ml
Spices for chicken	7 ml	15 ml	25 ml

Preparation

☐ Wipe the chicken portions with paper towels.

☐ Crush the biscuits.

Method

Brush the chicken portions with melted butter. Mix the biscuits, Parmesan cheese and seasonings together well and roll the chicken portions in the mixture. Place the chicken portions in a single layer in a baking pan and bake for 1 hour at 180 °C (350 °F) or until the chicken is cooked and golden brown.

Creamy potato bake

(12 servings; use 2 or 4 times the quantities for 24 or 48 servings)

12 cooked medium potatoes, sliced
125 ml crisply fried bacon
250 ml cream
150 ml grated Cheddar cheese
125 ml (60 g) fresh breadcrumbs
3 ml cayenne pepper
salt and freshly ground black pepper to taste

Method

Pack the potato slices in an ovenproof dish. Sprinkle the bacon over, then the cream, cheese and breadcrumbs. Season with cayenne pepper, salt and black pepper. Bake for 30-45 minutes at 180 °C (350 °F) or until golden brown.

Lemony cheese pudding

(12 small servings; use 2 or 4 times the quantities for 24 or 48 servings and make in separate containers)

1 packet sponge fingers
250 g smooth cottage cheese
175 ml natural yoghurt
30 ml lemon juice
10 ml grated lemon peel
1 packet lemon instant pudding
35 ml icing sugar

Method

Arrange sponge fingers in a pie dish. Mix the remaining ingredients, taking care not to stir too much. Spoon the mixture on top of the sponge fingers and chill until set.

Menu

Savoury chicken*
Creamy potato bake*
Stir-fried vegetables*
Green salad with crisp bacon

Lemony cheese pudding*

For 12 people you will need:

☐ salad ingredients:
300 g fresh young spinach (without hard ribs)
200 g button mushrooms
3 medium avocados
250 g bacon cubes, fried until crisp

Chicken with fruit chutney

Ingredients	12 servings	24 servings	48 servings
Worcester sauce	75 ml	100 ml	150 ml
Tomato sauce	75 ml	100 ml	150 ml
Mustard powder	10 ml	15 ml	30 ml
Curry powder	10 ml	15 ml	25 ml
Smooth apricot jam	75 ml	100 ml	150 ml
Fruit chutney	100 ml	150 ml	250 ml
Sugar	20 ml	30 ml	50 ml
Chicken portions (drumsticks, thighs or breasts)	12	24	48
Salt	10 ml	15 ml	25 ml

Preparation

☐ Pat the chicken dry with paper towels.

Method

Mix the Worcester sauce, tomato sauce, mustard powder, curry powder, apricot jam, chutney and sugar. Dip the chicken portions in the chutney sauce and pack them into an ovenproof dish. Pour the remaining sauce over. Season with salt. Cover the chicken and bake for 1-1½ hours at 180 °C (350 °F) or until cooked. Remove the covering and bake for 10-15 minutes until golden brown.

Lemony potatoes

(12 servings; use 2 or 4 times the quantities for 24 or 48 servings)

12 cooked medium potatoes, halved (keep warm)
50 ml lemon juice
15 ml grated lemon peel
50 ml butter
10 ml Aromat
freshly ground black pepper to taste

Method

Arrange potato halves in an ovenproof dish. Mix lemon juice, peel and butter in a small saucepan. Heat to boiling point. Pour over potatoes and season with Aromat and pepper.

Variations

Roast lemony potatoes: Parboil the potatoes, pour the melted lemon butter mixture over the potatoes and bake for 30 minutes, uncovered, at 180 °C (350 °F) or until golden brown. Season to taste.
Lemony potatoes with parsley: Sprinkle 30 ml chopped parsley over just before serving.
Lemony new potatoes: Allow 2 to 3 new potatoes a person, instead of 1 medium potato, and follow basic recipe.
Lemon-herb potatoes: Add 30 ml chopped fresh mixed herbs to the basic recipe.
Orange potatoes: Use orange juice and peel instead of lemon juice and peel.

Traditional bread pudding with custard

(6 servings; use 2, 4 or 8 times the quantities for 12, 24 or 48 servings, but 1½, 3 or 6 times the quantity of milk, and make in separate containers)

3 slices white bread, crusts removed and cut into triangles
350 ml milk
125 ml sugar
5 ml vanilla essence
3-4 eggs, separated
100 ml seedless raisins
25 ml castor sugar
60 ml smooth apricot jam

Method

Pack the bread in an ovenproof dish. Beat the milk, sugar, vanilla essence and egg yolks together. Sprinkle the raisins over the bread and pour the egg mixture over. Bake for 45 minutes at 160 °C (325 °F) until set. Whisk the egg whites and castor sugar to the soft peak stage. Spread apricot jam over the egg custard mixture, followed by stiffly whisked egg whites. Bake at 200 °C (400 °F) until light brown.

Menu

Chicken with fruit chutney*
Lemony potatoes*
Ratatouille with sweet peppers*
Coleslaw with yoghurt dressing*

Traditional bread pudding with custard*

Sweet-and-sour chicken

Ingredients	12 servings	24 servings	48 servings
Chicken portions (drumsticks, thighs or breasts)	12	24	48
Cooking oil	20 ml	50 ml	75 ml
Medium onions, chopped	200 g (2)	400 g (4)	800 g (8)
Canned pineapple pieces in syrup	2 x 410 g	3 x 410 g	6 x 410 g
Chicken stock or pineapple juice	100 ml	250 ml	500 ml
Soy sauce	20 ml	35 ml	75 ml
Brown grape vinegar	20 ml	35 ml	75 ml
Brown sugar	25 ml	40 ml	80 ml
Ground ginger	2 ml	5 ml	15 ml
Salt	10 ml	20 ml	40 ml
Green peppers, seeded and chopped	2	4	5
Red peppers, seeded and chopped	2	4	5
Cornflour	50 ml	125 ml	250 ml

Preparation

- ☐ Wipe the chicken portions with paper towels.
- ☐ Peel and chop the onions.
- ☐ Drain the pineapples, reserving the syrup.
- ☐ Seed and chop the sweet peppers.

Method

Brown the chicken portions in heated oil in a heavy-based saucepan. Add the onions and sauté until translucent. Add the heated pineapple syrup, chicken stock, soy sauce, vinegar, sugar, ginger and salt. Reduce the heat, cover with the lid and simmer for 1 hour or until the chicken is tender and cooked. Add the sweet peppers and pineapple pieces and simmer for a further 15 minutes. Thicken the sauce with the cornflour mixed to a paste with water.

Savoury rice

(12 servings; use 2 or 4 times the quantities for 24 or 48 servings)

400 g rice
1 large onion, finely chopped
1 carrot, finely grated
50 ml butter
5 ml Aromat
5 ml dried or 15 ml chopped fresh parsley

Method

Cook the rice according to the packet directions. Meanwhile, sauté the onion and carrot in heated butter until golden in colour. Mix the cooked rice with the onion mixture and fry lightly. Season with Aromat and parsley.

Apricot snow

(12 servings; use 2 or 4 times the quantities for 24 or 48 servings)

1 can (410 g) evaporated milk, chilled
2 packets (2 x 80 g) lemon jelly powder
10 ml lemon peel
1 can (410 g) apricots, drained and chopped
whipped cream and lemon peel for garnishing

Method

Whisk the evaporated milk until stiff and creamy. Dissolve the lemon jelly powder in a little water in a double boiler. Allow to cool slightly and fold into the evaporated milk with the peel and apricots. Leave the mixture in the refrigerator until set. The dessert can be spooned into individual dishes before placing it in the refrigerator. Garnish with whipped cream and lemon peel.

Menu

Sweet-and-sour chicken*
Savoury rice*
Buttered marrow
Mixed salad with cherry tomatoes and basil

Apricot snow*

For 12 people you will need:

- ☐ 2 kg marrow
- ☐ salad ingredients:
  - *1 medium butter lettuce*
  - *1 medium cucumber*
  - *24 cherry tomatoes*
  - *6 large or 12 small gherkins*
  - *24 basil leaves*

Fish pie with potatoes and cheese

Ingredients	12 servings	24 servings	48 servings
White fish, e.g. hake	1,2 kg	2,5 kg	5 kg
Fish or chicken stock	100 ml	200 ml	400 ml
Dry white wine	100 ml	200 ml	400 ml
Bay leaves	2	4	6
Carrots, coarsely grated	2	4	6
Medium onions, chopped	2	4	7
Garlic cloves, crushed	4	7	10
Butter	40 g	60 g	80 g
Salt	5 ml	10 ml	20 ml
White pepper	2 ml	5 ml	8 ml
Large potatoes	600 g (4)	1,2 kg (8)	2,4 kg (16)
Mild Cheddar cheese	200 g	350 g	650 g
Mild cheese sauce:			
Butter	50 g	100 g	200 g
Cake flour	60 ml (30 g)	120 ml (60 g)	250 ml (120 g)
Salt	3 ml	5 ml	7 ml
Milk	500 ml	1 litre	2 litres
Grated Cheddar cheese	100 ml	200 ml	400 ml

Preparation

☐ Blanch the fish in heated stock and wine to which bay leaves and carrots have been added. Drain and remove the skin and bones. Flake.
☐ Sauté the onions and garlic in heated butter until softened and translucent.
☐ Boil and slice the potatoes.
☐ Grate the cheese.

Method

Prepare the mild cheese sauce: Melt butter in a saucepan. Add the flour and salt and stir to make a roux. Add the milk, stirring constantly. Heat until the sauce is smooth and thick. Add the grated cheese and mix thoroughly.

Place the flaked fish in an ovenproof dish and spoon the sautéed onions and garlic on top. Season with salt and pepper. Arrange the potatoes on top of the onions. Pour the cheese sauce over the potatoes and sprinkle the cheese over. Bake for 20 minutes at 180 °C (350 °F) or until golden brown.

Chicken livers with rye bread

(12 servings; use 2 or 4 times the quantities for 24 or 48 servings)

50 g bacon, chopped
500 g chicken livers, chopped
2 onions, coarsely chopped
30 ml Worcester sauce
30 ml tomato sauce or tomato paste
10 ml dried or 30 ml chopped fresh basil
4 ml salt
2 ml freshly ground black pepper

Method

Fry the bacon in a pan until crisp. Add the chicken livers and onions and fry until the chicken livers are cooked. Add the remaining ingredients, reduce the heat and simmer for 10 minutes. Serve with rye bread.

Menu

Chicken livers with rye bread*

Fish pie with potatoes and cheese*
Buttered vegetables
Crisp green salad with bacon

Apple tart with cream

For 12 people you will need:

☐ 360 g young mealies
☐ 6 medium carrots
☐ 600 g green beans
☐ salad ingredients:
1 medium lettuce
½ English cucumber
3 medium avocados
250 g bacon, fried until crisp
☐ 2 apple tarts, each 225 mm in diameter (each serving 150 g)
☐ 350 ml cream

Sit-down dinners

Every now and then, there's an important event – a promotion, the christening of your first child, a wedding anniversary – that must be celebrated appropriately. And what better way to make the occasion unforgettable than by preparing an elegant sit-down meal?

Above from left: Potato salad with mustard mayonnaise (p. 89) and Chilled stewed dried peaches (menu, p. 65).
Front left: Beef olives with stir-fried vegetables (p. 60).
Front right: Pickled silverside with honey glaze (p. 65).

Beef olives with stir-fried vegetables

Ingredients	12 servings	24 servings	48 servings
Minced topside	250 g	500 g	1 kg
Fresh white breadcrumbs	180 ml (60 g)	350 ml (120 g)	750 ml (250 g)
Parsley, chopped	50 ml (20 g)	100 ml (40 g)	200 ml (75 g)
Medium onions, finely chopped	100 g (1)	100 g (1)	200 g (2)
Salt	3 ml	8 ml	20 ml
Freshly ground black pepper	pinch	2 ml	5 ml
Topside slices, cut 5 mm thick	1,3 kg (24 slices)	2,6 kg (48 slices)	5,2 kg (96 slices)
Rindless bacon	250 g	500 g	1 kg
Cooking oil	5 ml	10 ml	20 ml
Dry white wine	250 ml	500 ml	1 litre
Meat stock	500 ml	1 litre	2 litres
Bay leaves	2	4	8
Celery stalks	2	4	8
Parsley sprigs	2	4	8
Dried or chopped fresh thyme	2 ml or 5 ml	2 ml or 5 ml	5 ml or 15 ml
Lemon juice	50 ml	100 ml	200 ml
Stir-fried vegetables:			
Cooking oil	75 ml	150 ml	300 ml
Butter	25 ml	50 ml	100 ml
Leeks, thinly sliced	150 g (3)	300 g (6)	600 g (12)
Celery stalks, chopped	30 g (1)	90 g (3)	150 g (5)
Carrots, cut into julienne strips	500 g (5)	1 kg (10)	2 kg (20)
Green sweet peppers, seeded and cut into julienne strips	2	4	8
Red sweet peppers, seeded and cut into julienne strips	2	4	8
Mushrooms, sliced	250 g	500 g	1 kg
Salt	5 ml	12 ml	30 ml
Freshly ground black pepper	pinch	3 ml	10 ml

Preparation

- ☐ Chop the parsley.
- ☐ Peel and chop the onions.
- ☐ Slice the meat.
- ☐ Prepare the vegetables for the stir-fry:
  slice the leeks;
  chop the celery;
  cut the carrots into julienne strips;
  seed and cut the green and red sweet peppers into julienne strips;
  slice the mushrooms;
  cover the vegetables and chill.

Method

Prepare the filling: Mix the mince, breadcrumbs, parsley, onions and seasonings lightly with two forks.

Prepare the meat: Place the meat slices between two layers of plastic and beat them lightly with a meat mallet to make them slightly thinner. Place a bacon rasher on top of each meat slice. Place 12,5 ml filling on top of the bacon rasher. Roll up and secure with string, or toothpicks. Brown the meat in heated oil in a heavy-based saucepan. Add the heated wine and stock. Make a bouquet garni from the bay leaves, celery and parsley and add to

Menu

Fresh asparagus with hollandaise sauce*

Beef olives with stir-fried vegetables*
Parsley rice timbales*
Butter lettuce and cucumber with French dressing*

Cheesecake with black cherries

For 12 people you will need:

- ☐ 1,1 kg fresh asparagus
- ☐ salad ingredients:
  1 medium butter lettuce
  1 medium English cucumber
  4 medium green apples
- ☐ 1 large cheesecake
- ☐ 2 large cans black cherries

the meat. Add the thyme and lemon juice. Cover with the lid, reduce the heat and simmer for 1-1½ hours or until the beef olives are tender.

Prepare the vegetables: Heat the oil and butter in a pan. Add the leeks and sauté lightly. Add the remaining vegetables and sauté for a few minutes. Season with salt and freshly ground black pepper. Serve with the beef olives.

Menu

Mushroom quiche*

Rainbow-larded beef pot roast*
Roasted new potatoes
Glazed pumpkin slices
Buttered baby marrows
Green salad with red sweet peppers

Brandied peaches*

For 12 people you will need:

- ☐ 1,4 kg new potatoes
- ☐ 2,4 kg pumpkin
- ☐ 2 kg baby marrows
- ☐ salad ingredients:
  300 g young spinach leaves
  *750 g button mushrooms, marinated**
  1 medium onion
  2 medium red sweet peppers
  2 celery stalks

Rainbow-larded beef pot roast

Ingredients	12 servings	24 servings	48 servings
Beef for pot-roasting: bolo, topside, silverside or aitchbone	2,5 kg	2 x 2,5 kg	4 x 2,5 kg
Large carrots, cut into strips	100 g (1)	200 g (2)	300 g (3)
Celery stalks, cut into strips	2	4	8
Speck, cut into thin strips	50 g	100 g	200 g
Cooking oil	50 ml	100 ml	200 ml
Medium onions, finely chopped	300 g (3)	600 g (6)	1 kg (10)
Garlic cloves, crushed	4	8	16
Salt	10 ml	20 ml	30 ml
Freshly ground black pepper	3 ml	6 ml	10 ml
Dried or chopped fresh rosemary	3 ml or 10 ml	5 ml or 15 ml	10 ml or 30 ml
Meat stock	500 ml	1 litre	2 litres
Cake flour	30 ml (15 g)	50 ml (25 g)	80 ml (40 g)
Chopped fresh parsley	75 ml	150 ml	250 ml

Preparation

- ☐ Cut the carrots, celery and speck into thin strips.
- ☐ Lard the meat, with the grain, using carrots, celery and speck. Secure with string at regular intervals.
- ☐ Peel and chop the onions finely.
- ☐ Peel and crush the garlic cloves.
- ☐ Chop the parsley.

Method

Brown the meat in the heated oil in a heavy-based saucepan. Add the onions and garlic and sauté until the onions are translucent. Add the seasonings and heated stock. Cover with the lid, reduce the heat and simmer for 2-2½ hours or until the meat is tender. Thicken the gravy with the flour mixed to a paste with water. Remove the string and carve into thin slices. Pour the gravy over the meat and garnish with chopped parsley.

Flat rib roll with cheese stuffing

Ingredients	12 servings	24 servings	48 servings
Boned flat rib of beef (for roll)	3 kg	2 x 3 kg	4 x 3 kg
French mustard	20 ml	40 ml	80 ml
Salt	10 ml	20 ml	40 ml
Freshly ground black pepper	5 ml	10 ml	20 ml
Chopped fresh parsley	75 ml	150 ml	250 ml
Minced beef	150 g	300 g	600 g
Onions, chopped	100 g (1)	200 g (2)	400 g (4)
Eggs	1	2	4
Celery stalks, chopped	2	4	8
Cake flour	30 ml (15 g)	60 ml (30 g)	125 ml (60 g)
Grated Cheddar cheese	125 ml	250 ml	500 ml
Cooking oil	50 ml	100 ml	200 ml
Medium onions, chopped	100 g (1)	200 g (2)	400 g (4)
Meat stock	500 ml	1 litre	2 litres
Dried or chopped fresh basil	5 ml or 15 ml	10 ml or 30 ml	20 ml or 60 ml
Cake flour	30 ml (15 g)	60 ml (30 g)	125 ml (60 g)

Menu

Avocado with crisp bacon*

Flat rib roll with cheese stuffing*
Brown rice
Cauliflower with nutmeg
Buttered patty pans
Green salad with bean sprouts

Cheese board with savoury biscuits

For 12 people you will need:
- ☐ 400 g brown rice
- ☐ 2 kg cauliflower
- ☐ 1,2 kg patty pans
- ☐ salad ingredients:
  - *200 g frisée lettuce*
  - *12 gherkins*
  - *½ English cucumber*
  - *200 g bean sprouts (chickpea sprouts)*
- ☐ cheese board:
  - *300 g Cheddar or Gouda cheese*
  - *200 g Blaauwkrantz cheese*
- ☐ 36 (3 kinds x 12 each) savoury biscuits

Preparation

☐ Remove excess fat from the meat. Spread mustard over the inside of the meat and season with half the salt and pepper.

☐ Mix the parsley, mince, onions, eggs and celery thoroughly and spread it over the mustard layer. Sprinkle the flour and cheese over.

☐ Roll up the meat and secure it every 25 mm with string.

Method

Brown the meat in heated oil in a heavy-based saucepan. Add the onions and sauté until translucent. Add the heated stock and basil, cover with the lid, reduce the heat and simmer for 2-2½ hours or until the meat is tender. Thicken the gravy with the flour mixed to a paste with water. Remove the string and carve the meat thinly.

Avocado with crisp bacon

(12 servings; use 2 or 4 times the quantities for 24 or 48 servings)

6 ripe avocados, peeled and stoned
30 ml lemon juice
200 g bacon, cubed
fresh herbs for garnishing

Method

Cut the avocados lengthways into strips. Sprinkle lemon juice over and arrange the avocado strips on individual plates.

Fry the bacon cubes until crisp, drain and sprinkle over the avocado. Garnish with fresh herbs.

Rolled leg of lamb with rosemary

Ingredients	12 servings	24 servings	48 servings
Boned leg of lamb	2 kg	4 kg	7,5 kg
Salt	10 ml	20 ml	40 ml
Freshly ground black pepper	3 ml	5 ml	10 ml
Gelatine	15 ml	30 ml	60 ml
Lemon peel	7 ml	15 ml	30 ml
Dried or chopped fresh rosemary	5 ml or 15 ml	15 ml or 45 ml	20 ml or 60 ml
Rosemary basting sauce:			
Dry white wine	100 ml	150 ml	250 ml
Lemon juice	20 ml	30 ml	60 ml
Lemon peel	5 ml	8 ml	15 ml
Cooking oil	30 ml	50 ml	100 ml
Salt	1 ml	2 ml	3 ml
Freshly ground black pepper	0,5 ml	1 ml	2 ml

Preparation

☐ Sprinkle half the salt and pepper, as well as the gelatine, lemon peel and rosemary, over the inside of the meat. Roll up the meat and secure at 25 mm intervals with string.

☐ Mix all the basting sauce ingredients.

Method

Season the meat with the remaining salt and pepper and place it on the rack of an oven-roasting pan. Oven-roast at 160 °C (325 °F): 20 to 25 minutes per 500 g plus 20 minutes extra for medium; 25 to 30 minutes per 500 g plus 25 minutes extra for well done.

During cooking, baste the meat often with the basting sauce. Leave meat to rest in a warming drawer for 10 minutes to facilitate carving.

Remove the string and carve thinly. Serve cold or hot.

Gingered shrimp fingers

(24 large servings; use ½ or 2 times the quantities for 12 or 48 servings)

500 g shrimps, shells and veins removed
1 medium onion
5 ml chopped fresh ginger root
2 ml salt
freshly ground black pepper to taste
2 egg whites
15 slices day-old white bread, crusts removed
250 ml dried breadcrumbs
cooking oil for shallow-frying
dill sprig for garnishing

Method

Place the shrimps, onion, ginger root, salt and pepper in a food processor. Switch on the food processor and add the egg whites, one at a time. Mix until smooth. Slice the bread lengthways into fingers, spread shrimp mixture on both sides and roll the shrimp fingers in breadcrumbs. Refrigerate for 30 minutes. Fry the shrimp fingers in heated cooking oil until golden brown. Garnish with a dill sprig.

Tip

☐ Instead of ginger root, use 5 ml French mustard.

Menu

Gingered shrimp fingers*
Green salad

Rolled leg of lamb with rosemary*
Roast lemony potatoes*
Green beans and bacon
Orange carrots*

Fruit sorbet with ginger biscuits

For 12 people you will need:

☐ salad ingredients:
100 g watercress
250 g mixed salad leaves
12 spring onions
12 fresh green asparagus, poached

☐ 1,2 kg green beans
☐ 125 g bacon
☐ 1,2 litres fruit sorbet
☐ 12 ginger biscuits

Pot-roast shoulder of lamb with spinach stuffing

Ingredients	12 servings	24 servings	48 servings
Boned shoulder of lamb, whole	2 x 1 kg	4 x 1 kg	8 x 1 kg
Salt	10 ml	15 ml	25 ml
Freshly ground black pepper	3 ml	7 ml	10 ml
Cooking oil	10 ml	20 ml	30 ml
Butter	10 ml	30 ml	60 ml
Dry white wine	500 ml	750 ml	1 litre
Meat stock	500 ml	750 ml	1 litre
Dried or chopped fresh basil	3 ml or 10 ml	7 ml or 20 ml	15 ml or 45 ml
Cake flour	15 ml (5 g)	30 ml (15 g)	50 ml (25 g)
Spinach stuffing:			
Rindless bacon, finely chopped	75 g	150 g	250 g
Shallots or leeks, chopped	2	3	5
Garlic cloves, crushed	3	6	8
Mushrooms, finely chopped	150 g	250 g	500 g
Dried or chopped fresh basil	3 ml or 10 ml	3 ml or 10 ml	5 ml or 15 ml
Lemon juice	5 ml	15 ml	25 ml
Fresh spinach, stalks removed, shredded	250 g	500 g	1 kg
Fresh breadcrumbs	75 ml (25 g)	150 ml (50 g)	300 ml (100 g)
Sour cream (optional)	30 ml.	60 ml	100 ml
Eggs	1	1	2
Salt	3 ml	6 ml	10 ml
Freshly ground black pepper	1 ml	3 ml	5 ml

Preparation

☐ Prepare the spinach stuffing: Fry the bacon until crisp. Add the shallots and garlic and sauté for a few minutes. Add the mushrooms and fry until soft. Add the basil and lemon juice. Remove from the stove. Blanch the spinach and add to the mushroom mixture. Add the breadcrumbs, sour cream, eggs, salt and pepper and mix thoroughly.

Method

Prepare the meat: Place the meat, fat side down, on a wooden board. Season the meat with half the salt and pepper. Spoon the stuffing in the centre of the lamb shoulder and spread it evenly over the meat to about 10 mm from the sides. Roll up and secure with string at regular intervals. Brown the meat in heated oil and butter. Add the heated white wine and stock, as well as the seasonings. Cover with the lid, reduce the heat and simmer for 1½-2 hours or until the meat is tender. Thicken the gravy with the flour mixed to a paste with water. Remove the string and carve the meat thinly.

Menu

Marinated salmon trout*

Pot-roast shoulder of lamb with spinach stuffing*
Savoury rice
French green beans
Baby carrots with parsley
Oven-baked pickling onions*

Chocolate mousse*

For 12 people you will need:

☐ 400 g rice
☐ 1,2 kg green beans
☐ 1,2 kg frozen baby carrots

Pickled silverside with honey glaze

Ingredients	12 servings	24 servings	48 servings
Pickled silverside	3 kg	2 x 3 kg	4 x 3 kg
Black peppercorns	6	12	20
Whole cloves	4	8	16
Bay leaves	2	4	8
Medium onions, whole	200 g (2)	400 g (4)	800 g (8)
Carrots, sliced	100 g (1)	200 g (2)	400 g (4)
Honey glaze:			
Clear apple juice	125 ml	250 ml	500 ml
Brown sugar	50 ml	75 ml	150 ml
Honey	75 ml	100 ml	200 ml
Mustard powder	12 ml	20 ml	40 ml

Preparation

☐ Peel the onions.
☐ Peel and slice the carrots.

Method

Prepare the meat: Place the meat in a large saucepan and cover with cold water. Place the peppercorns, cloves and bay leaves in a muslin bag and add to the meat with the onions and carrots. Heat to boiling point, cover with the lid, reduce the heat and simmer for 2-2½ hours or until the meat is tender.

Prepare the honey glaze: Mix all the ingredients in a small saucepan. Heat over low heat until the sugar has dissolved. Remove the meat from the saucepan, place it on the rack of a roasting pan and roast for 20 minutes at 160 °C (325 °F), basting constantly with the honey glaze. Carve the meat thinly and serve either hot or cold.

Biltong pâté

(12 servings; use 2 or 4 times the quantities for 24 or 48 servings)

300 g grated biltong
30 ml lemon juice
15 ml lemon peel
300 ml sour cream
375 ml cream cheese
salt and freshly ground black pepper to taste
herb sprigs
butter

Method

Place all the ingredients, except the butter, in a food processor and mix until smooth. Place the pâté in a small bowl, smooth the surface and place a herb sprig on top.

Heat the butter and allow it to cook slowly until foamy. Skim off the foam and pour off the clarified butter carefully, ensuring that the sediment remains behind. Pour the hot butter over the pâté and chill until the butter layer has set.

Menu

Biltong pâté* with Melba toast

Pickled silverside with honey glaze*
Potato salad*
Chilled stewed dried peaches
Young spinach salad with croutons*

Fruit salad with granadilla coulis

For 12 people you will need:

☐ 24 slices Melba toast
☐ 500 g dried peaches
☐ salad ingredients:
300 g young spinach (without tough stalks)
250 g bean sprouts
36 cherry tomatoes
☐ fruit salad ingredients:
4 large oranges
2 large mangoes
1 small pineapple
25 ml chopped mint
12,5 ml lemon juice
125 ml pineapple juice
50 ml sherry
☐ pulp of 12 granadillas for coulis

Rolled breast of pork with fruit sauce

Ingredients	12 servings	24 servings	48 servings
Boned breast of pork, rind and excess fat removed	1,8 kg	3 kg	3 x 2 kg
French mustard	15 ml	25 ml	45 ml
Salt	8 ml	15 ml	30 ml
Freshly ground black pepper	2 ml	3 ml	5 ml
Dried apricots, finely chopped	125 g	250 g	500 g
Cooking oil	20 ml	30 ml	50 ml
Apricot juice	150 ml	250 ml	500 ml
White meat stock	250 ml	500 ml	1 litre
Fruit sauce:			
Brown sugar	75 ml	150 ml	300 ml
White wine vinegar	50 ml	100 ml	200 ml
Canned pie apples	1 x 410 g	1 x 840 g	2 x 840 g
Canned apricot halves	1 x 410 g	1 x 840 g	2 x 840 g
Sultanas	60 ml	125 ml	250 ml
Mustard powder	2 ml	3 ml	5 ml
French mustard	15 ml	25 ml	50 ml
Cornflour	about 10 ml	about 20 ml	about 35-40 ml

Preparation

☐ Spread mustard over the inside of the meat and season with half the salt and pepper. Place the dried apricots on top of the mustard, roll up the meat and secure at 25 mm intervals with string.

☐ Soak the sultanas for the fruit sauce in rooibos tea until plump.

Method

Brown the meat in heated oil in a heavy-based saucepan. Add the heated apricot juice, stock, and the remaining salt and pepper. Cover with the lid, reduce the heat and simmer for 1½ hours or until the meat is tender. Remove the string and carve the meat thinly.

Prepare the fruit sauce: Heat the brown sugar and vinegar until the sugar has dissolved. Add the pie apples, apricots, drained sultanas and mustard. Thicken the sauce with the cornflour mixed to a paste with water, if necessary. Pour the sauce over the meat slices and serve immediately.

Tips

☐ Soaked dried fruit can be used instead of the canned apricot halves.

☐ Rib of pork can be used instead of breast of pork.

Above left: Green salad with red sweet peppers (menu, p. 61). Above right: Brandied peaches (p. 94). Front: Rainbow-larded beef pot roast (p. 61), served with Roasted new potatoes (menu, p. 61).

Menu

Crudités with herbed cottage cheese

Rolled breast of pork with fruit sauce*
Hot potato salad with Blaauwkrantz cheese sauce*
Marinated mushrooms*
Crisp green salad with nuts

Melon in port

For 12 people you will need:

☐ crudités:
6 medium carrots
200 g cauliflower florets
200 g mushrooms
200 g young mealies
500 ml herbed cottage cheese

☐ salad ingredients:
1 medium lettuce
1 medium cucumber
250 g bean sprouts
120 g nuts

☐ 3 medium sweet melons

☐ 80 ml port

Chicken pie with sour cream crust

Ingredients	12 servings	24 servings	48 servings
Cooked chickens	3	5	8
Grated nutmeg	15 ml	25 ml	35 ml
Whole cloves	4	8	16
Black peppercorns	4	8	16
Chicken stock	500 ml	1 litre	1,5 litres
Brown wine vinegar	75 ml	125 ml	200 ml
Worcester sauce	30 ml	45 ml	60 ml
Salt	7 ml	10 ml	15 ml
White pepper	pinch	2 ml	5 ml
Eggs, beaten	1	2	3
Fresh breadcrumbs	75 ml	125 ml	200 ml
Sour cream crust:			
Cake flour	500 ml (250 g)	750 ml (375 g)	1,5 litres (750 g)
Baking powder	10 ml	15 ml	30 ml
Salt	2,5 ml	5 ml	10 ml
Butter	175 g	350 g	700 g
Sour cream	250 ml	375 ml	750 ml

Preparation

☐ Prepare the sour cream crust: Sift the dry ingredients together. Rub in the butter with your fingertips. Add the sour cream and mix to make a soft, pliable pastry. Refrigerate the pastry overnight.

☐ Season the chickens with salt and pepper to taste. Place the chickens in a baking bag and bake for 1-1½ hours at 180 °C (350 °F) or until cooked.

☐ Beat the eggs.

Method

Bone the chickens and cut the flesh into bite-sized pieces. Add the nutmeg, cloves, peppercorns, stock, vinegar, Worcester sauce, salt and pepper and simmer for 10 minutes. Allow to cool slightly and stir in the egg. (Reserve a little of the beaten egg for brushing the pastry.) Place the meat mixture into a pie dish and sprinkle the breadcrumbs over. Roll out the pastry to 5 mm thick and place it on top of the meat mixture. Brush the pastry with egg. Bake for 25 minutes in a preheated oven at 200 °C (400 °F) or until golden brown.

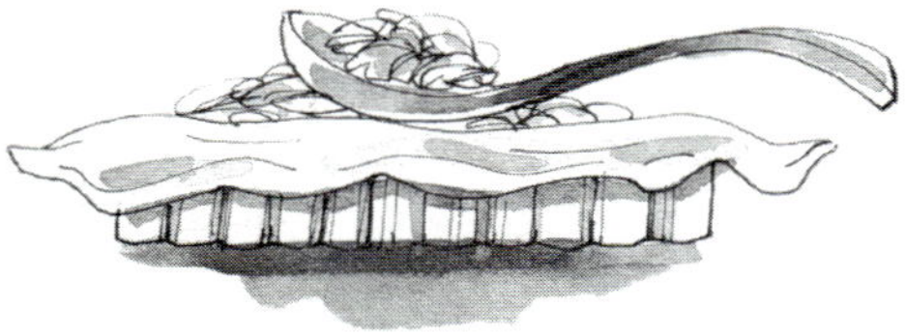

Savoury rice with red sweet peppers

(12 servings; use 2 or 4 times the quantities for 24 or 48 servings)

400 g white rice
15 ml salt
1 medium onion, finely chopped
10 ml butter
¼ pineapple, cut into 5 mm cubes
2 red sweet peppers, cut into 5 mm cubes
30 ml chopped fresh parsley

Method

Boil the rice according to the instructions on the package, using 15 ml salt. Sauté the onion in heated butter until transparent. Add the pineapple and sweet peppers and fry for a few minutes. Add the onion mixture to the cooked rice and mix thoroughly. Garnish with chopped parsley.

Menu

Vegetable soup with whole-wheat bread

Chicken pie with sour cream crust*
Savoury rice with red sweet peppers*
Green beans with onions and bacon*
Pumpkin with orange sauce*

Baked pears with cream*

For 12 people you will need:

☐ 2,4 litres vegetable soup
☐ 1 whole-wheat loaf (20 slices)

Green beans with onions and bacon

(12 servings; use 2 or 4 times the quantities for 24 or 48 servings)

1,2 kg young green beans, halved
150 ml meat stock
250 g bacon, cubed
18 pickling onions, peeled and a cross cut in the root end

Method
Boil the green beans in heated meat stock for 20 minutes, until tender but still crisp. Place the bacon in a cold pan and heat it gradually. Fry the bacon until crisp, add the pickling onions and fry for a further 5 minutes. Drain the beans and mix with the bacon and pickling onions.

Tip
□ The pickling onions can be blanched beforehand.

Pumpkin with orange sauce

(12 servings; use 2 or 4 times the quantities for 24 and 48 servings)

2 kg "boer" pumpkin cubes
60 ml orange juice
20 ml grated orange peel
5 ml lemon juice
20 ml butter
100 ml brown sugar
1 ml salt

Method
Boil the pumpkin in a little water over low heat for 30 minutes, or until almost tender.

Add the orange juice, peel, lemon juice, butter, sugar and salt. Increase the heat and allow the pumpkin to caramelise slightly. Garnish with extra orange peel.

Variation
Pumpkin with ginger syrup: Omit orange juice and peel and use 80-100 ml chopped preserved ginger and syrup.

Baked pears with cream

(12 servings; use 2 or 4 times the quantities for 24 or 48 servings, and make batter in separate containers)

1 can (410 g) pears, drained
125 ml sugar
4 eggs
375 ml cake flour
12 ml baking powder
1 ml salt
60 ml butter
160 ml milk
5 ml vanilla essence

360 ml fresh cream or custard

Syrup
160 ml golden syrup
100 ml butter

Method
Arrange pears in an ovenproof dish. Beat the sugar and eggs thoroughly. Sift the dry ingredients together and add the egg mixture. Melt the butter and add to the milk. Add to the flour mixture with the vanilla essence. Mix to a smooth batter. Pour over the pears and bake for 15-20 minutes at 180 °C (350 °F) or until golden brown. Melt the syrup and butter in a small saucepan and pour over the cake mixture as soon as it comes from the oven. Serve the pears with cream or custard.

Lemon chicken with sesame seeds

Ingredients	12 servings	24 servings	48 servings
Chicken portions (drum-sticks, thighs or breasts)	12	24	48
Cooking oil	50 ml	80 ml	150 ml
Sesame seeds	100 ml	175 ml	250 ml
Butter	75 g	100 g	200 g
Sugar	125 ml	250 ml	500 ml
Chicken stock	150 ml	300 ml	600 ml
Lemon juice	100 ml	200 ml	300 ml
Salt	5 ml	10 ml	15 ml
Cornflour	25 ml	50 ml	100 ml
Cold water	50 ml	100 ml	150 ml

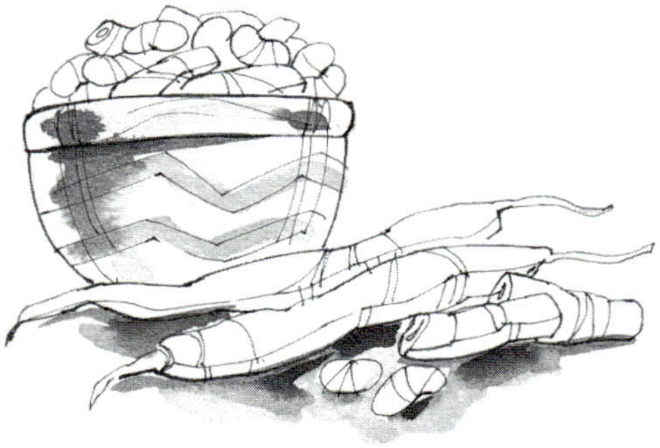

Preparation

☐ Wipe the chicken portions dry with paper towels.
☐ Squeeze out the lemon juice.

Method

Fry the chicken in heated oil over low heat until golden brown and cooked. Sprinkle the sesame seeds over and allow to cool. Melt the butter and add the sugar. Heat until the sugar caramelises. Add the stock and lemon juice and cook until the caramel has dissolved. Add the salt. Thicken the sauce with the cornflour mixed to a paste with water. Spoon the caramel sauce over the chicken and serve immediately.

Three-bean salad

(12 servings; use 2 or 4 times the quantities for 24 or 48 servings)

1 can (410 g) butter beans
1 can (410 g) beans in tomato sauce
400 g sliced green beans, blanched
1 onion, finely chopped
125 ml brown sugar
50 ml cooking oil
125 ml white grape vinegar
100 ml water
10 ml mustard powder

Method

Mix all the beans with the chopped onion. Place the brown sugar, oil, vinegar, water and mustard powder in a small saucepan and heat to boiling point. Allow to cool slightly and pour over the beans. Serve chilled.

Menu

Deep-fried haddock

Lemon chicken with sesame seeds*
Potato salad
Three-bean salad*
Fresh green mixed salad
Pineapple salad

Fruit salad

For 12 people you will need:

☐ 1,5 kg haddock
☐ potato salad:
1,8 kg potatoes
360 ml sour cream
100 ml chopped spring onions
250 g bacon, fried until crisp
☐ salad ingredients:
1 large butter lettuce
1 English cucumber
100 g lucerne sprouts
200 g mangetout
2 medium pineapples
☐ fruit salad ingredients:
500 g strawberries
4 medium kiwi fruit
3 medium papinos
500 ml natural yoghurt

Fish pie with asparagus

Ingredients	12 servings	24 servings	48 servings
White fish, cubed	1,2 kg	2 kg	4 kg
Medium onions, finely chopped	400 g (4)	600 g (6)	1 kg (10)
Butter	125 g	250 g	400 g
Canned asparagus, drained	2 x 450 g	4 x 450 g	6 x 450 g
Cheddar cheese, grated	500 g	1 kg	1,5 kg
Fresh cream	250 ml	400 ml	750 ml
Salt	10 ml	15 ml	25 ml
White pepper	3 ml	8 ml	10 ml
Potato topping:			
Potatoes, peeled and cubed	1,2 kg (8)	2,4 kg (16)	4,5 kg (30)
Milk	100 ml	200 ml	400 ml
Butter	100 ml	200 ml	350 ml
Salt	5 ml	10 ml	15 ml
White pepper	2 ml	5 ml	8 ml
Grated Cheddar cheese	100 g	180 g	350 g
Spring onions, chopped	50 ml	100 ml	200 ml

Preparation

☐ Peel and chop the onions finely.
☐ Grate the cheese.
☐ Potato topping: Boil the potatoes until tender, mash them and add milk, butter and seasonings. Mix thoroughly with the cheese and spring onions.

Method

Fry the fish and onions in heated butter until the fish is done. Add the asparagus, cheese, cream and seasonings and place in an ovenproof dish. Spoon the potato topping on top of the fish and bake for 20 minutes in a preheated oven at 180 °C (350 °F) or until golden brown.

Broccoli with toasted almonds

(12 servings; use 2 or 4 times the quantities for 24 or 48 servings)

100 ml boiling water
7 ml salt
1,4 kg broccoli, broken into florets
20 ml butter
75 g toasted blanched almonds

Method

Heat the water and salt to boiling point and boil the broccoli for 10-15 minutes. Drain, add butter and mix lightly Place in a serving dish and sprinkle the nuts over just before serving.

Baby marrows with tomato

(12 servings; use 2 or 4 times the quantities for 24 or 48 servings)

1 large onion, cut into rings
10 ml butter
1,4 kg baby marrows cut into 20 mm lengths
5 ml salt
freshly ground black pepper
3 tomatoes, peeled and cubed
5 ml dried or 15 ml chopped fresh basil
5 ml sugar

Method

Sauté the onion in heated butter until translucent. Add the rest of the ingredients and heat to boiling point. Reduce the heat, cover with the lid and simmer for 20 minutes or until the baby marrows are tender.

Menu

Fish pie with asparagus*
Broccoli with toasted almonds*
Baby marrows with tomato*
Green salad with cottage cheese and nuts*

Caramel dumplings*

Nothing but the best

It's time to pull out all the stops, put your best foot forward and make your guests gasp in amazement . . . because not one of these special dinner menus will be easily forgotten. Each dish has been carefully planned and prepared to ensure the ultimate in taste, flavour and appearance. And the finishing touches and garnishing of dishes are the final, indispensable step.

Above from left: Green salad with fresh herbs (menu, p. 85) and Oven-baked loin of pork with orange (p. 85). Front left: Butterflied leg of lamb with caper butter topping (p. 86). Front right: Young beets with youngberry sauce (p. 91).

Fillet with creamy paprika sauce

Ingredients	12 servings	24 servings	48 servings
Beef fillet	2,2 kg	4 kg	7,5 kg
Rindless streaky bacon	2 x 250 g	4 x 250 g	4 x 500 g
Creamy paprika sauce:			
Brown mushrooms, sliced	350 g	600 g	1,2 kg
Butter	50 ml	100 ml	200 ml
Paprika	8 ml	12 ml	20 ml
Cream	250 ml	400 ml	800 ml
Milk	250 ml	400 ml	800 ml
Lemon juice	15 ml	30 ml	50 ml
Salt	4 ml	8 ml	15 ml
Freshly ground black pepper	2 ml	3 ml	5 ml
Cake flour	15 ml (5 g)	30 ml (15 g)	60 ml (30 g)

Preparation

☐ Slice the mushrooms.

Method

Place the meat on the rack of an oven-roasting pan and lard it with bacon rashers (place the bacon over the fillet). Oven-roast the fillet at 160 °C (325 °F): 15-20 minutes per 500 g plus 15 minutes extra for rare; 20-25 minutes per 500 g plus 20 minutes for medium; 25-30 minutes per 500 g plus 25 minutes extra for well done.

Prepare the creamy paprika sauce: Fry the mushrooms in heated butter until cooked. Add all the ingredients except the flour and simmer for 10 minutes over low heat. Thicken the sauce with the flour mixed to a paste with water. Cut the meat into 25 mm thick slices and serve on croutes, with sauce.

Crêpes suzettes

(24 servings; use ½ or 2 times the quantities for 12 or 48 servings)

750 ml (360 g) cake flour
10 ml baking powder
2 ml salt
3-4 eggs, beaten
3 x 375 ml milk (or equal quantities milk and water)
15 ml lemon juice
90 ml cooking oil

Orange Sauce

1,5 litres fresh orange juice
50 ml orange peel
50 g butter
100 ml sugar
100 ml orange liqueur or brandy

Method

Sift the dry ingredients together. Beat the eggs, milk, lemon juice and oil together thoroughly. Add to the dry ingredients and mix to a smooth dropping consistency. Fry pancakes in a small pan (20 cm diameter – makes about 30 pancakes). Keep warm.

Prepare the orange sauce: Heat all the ingredients, except the orange liqueur, in a saucepan.

Fold the pancakes into triangles and arrange them in a heated serving dish. Pour the orange sauce over. Heat the orange liqueur, flame and pour it over the pancakes. Serve immediately.

Tip

☐ The pancakes freeze very successfully.

Menu

Chicken-filled phyllo parcels*

Fillet with creamy paprika sauce*
Croutes
Fresh asparagus
Buttered young mealies and carrots

Crêpes suzettes*

For 12 people you will need:

☐ croutes:
1 white loaf (20 slices = 20 fried bread rounds)
☐ 1,1 kg fresh asparagus
☐ 800 g young mealies
☐ 800 g frozen baby carrots

Mustard-topped beef rump

Ingredients	12 servings	24 servings	48 servings
Whole beef rump	2 kg	3,5 kg	2 x 3 kg
Salt	10 ml	15 ml	30 ml
Freshly ground black pepper	2 ml	5 ml	10 ml
Mustard topping:			
Chopped fresh parsley	50 ml	100 ml	200 ml
Garlic cloves, crushed	2	4	7
French mustard	40 ml	80 ml	150 ml
Melted butter	40 ml	80 ml	150 ml
Fresh breadcrumbs	100 ml	200 ml	400 ml
Parmesan cheese (optional)	25 g	50 g	90 g

Preparation

☐ Chop the parsley.
☐ Peel and crush the garlic cloves.
☐ Prepare the breadcrumbs.
☐ Mix all the ingredients for the mustard topping thoroughly.

Method

Place the meat on the rack of an oven-roasting pan. Season with salt and pepper. Oven-roast at 160 °C (325 °F): 15-20 minutes per 500 g for rare; 20-25 minutes per 500 g for medium; 25-30 minutes per 500 g for well done.

Remove the meat from the oven, spread the mustard topping over it evenly and return it to the oven for a further 30 minutes, or until the topping is golden brown. Place the meat in a warming drawer for 10 minutes to facilitate carving. Carve the meat thinly. Serve cold or hot.

Potato croquettes

(12 servings; use 2 or 4 times the quantities for 24 or 48 servings)

700 ml mashed potatoes
15 ml chopped parsley
10 ml lemon peel
2 ml salt
250 ml dried breadcrumbs
1-2 eggs, beaten
cooking oil for deep-frying

WHITE SAUCE
40 ml butter
40 ml (20 g) cake flour
250 ml milk
salt and pepper to taste

Method

Prepare the white sauce by melting the butter and stirring in the flour. Add the milk gradually, and cook over low heat until the sauce thickens, stirring constantly. Season to taste. Add all the ingredients, except the crumbs and eggs, and mix well. Shape into rolls. Roll in breadcrumbs, then egg, and again in breadcrumbs. Refrigerate for 30 minutes. Deep-fry the croquettes until golden brown. Drain on paper towels and serve immediately.

Menu

Mock chicken drumsticks peri-peri*

Mustard-topped beef rump*
Potato croquettes*
Ratatouille with red sweet peppers*
Mixed salad with tomato and basil

Brandied peaches* with cream

For 12 people you will need:
☐ salad ingredients:
300 g young spinach (tough stalks removed)
12 gherkins
6 small tomatoes
12 basil leaves
☐ 350 ml cream

Pot-roast beef with creamy walnut sauce

Ingredients	12 servings	24 servings	48 servings
Bolo, topside or thick flank	1 x 2 kg	2 x 2 kg	4 x 2 kg
Garlic cloves, crushed	3	6	12
Chopped fresh parsley	30 ml	50 ml	100 ml
Softened butter	30 ml	50 ml	100 ml
Cooking oil	30 ml	60 ml	120 ml
Fresh pickling onions	12	24	48
Celery stalks	2	4	8
Brandy	30 ml	60 ml	120 ml
Meat stock	250 ml	500 ml	1 litre
Salt	10 ml	20 ml	30 ml
Freshly ground black pepper	3 ml	5 ml	10 ml
Dried or chopped fresh rosemary	5 ml or 15 ml	10 ml or 30 ml	20 ml or 60 ml
Cake flour	25 ml (12 g)	50 ml (25 g)	100 ml (80 g)
Walnuts, chopped	50 g	100 g	200 g
Cream	80 ml	150 ml	300 ml
French mustard	15 ml	30 ml	60 ml

Preparation

☐ Tie meat with string at regular intervals. Mix the garlic, parsley and butter to a paste. Make small incisions in the surface of the meat and fill them with the butter mixture.

☐ Peel the pickling onions.

☐ Chop the walnuts.

Method

Brown the meat in the heated oil in a heavy-based saucepan. Add the pickling onions and celery and sauté until the onions are translucent. Heat the brandy, flame and add to the meat with the heated stock and the seasonings. Cover with the lid, reduce the heat and simmer for 2-2½ hours or until the meat is tender. Thicken the sauce with the flour mixed to a paste with water. Add the walnuts, cream and mustard and mix thoroughly. Remove the string and carve the meat thinly. Pour the sauce over and serve immediately.

Pumpkin slices with honeyed orange sauce

(12 servings; use 2 or 4 times the quantities for 24 or 48 servings)

2,4 kg "boer" pumpkin, cut into 30 mm slices, pips removed
10 ml salt
60 ml butter

Honeyed Orange Sauce
60-80 ml honey
120 ml orange juice
10 ml lemon juice
5 ml ground ginger

Method

Arrange the pumpkin slices in a single layer in an ovenproof dish. Season with salt and dot with butter. Cover and bake for 30-40 minutes at 180 °C (350 °F). Turn once during cooking. Prepare the honeyed orange sauce by heating all the ingredients in a small saucepan. Pour over the pumpkin slices and bake for a further 10 minutes, uncovered, until glazed.

Menu

Marinated biltong on watercress*

Pot-roast beef with creamy walnut sauce*
Fried rice*
Pumpkin slices with honeyed orange sauce*
Buttered broccoli
Fresh green salad with avocado

Mock cheesecake with gooseberries*

For 12 people you will need:

☐ 2 kg broccoli

☐ salad ingredients:
300 g young spinach leaves (tough stalks removed)
2 medium green sweet peppers
12 chives
3 medium avocados

Beef pie with buttermilk pastry

Ingredients	12 servings	24 servings	48 servings
Boned neck or shin of beef, cut into 20 mm cubes	2 kg	4 kg	8 kg
Cooking oil	40 ml	80 ml	150 ml
Medium onions, finely chopped	200 g (2)	300 g (3)	500 g (5)
Garlic cloves, crushed	2	4	8
Salt	12 ml	20 ml	35 ml
Freshly ground black pepper	3 ml	5 ml	10 ml
Dried or chopped mixed fresh herbs	5 ml or 15 ml	15 ml or 45 ml	25 ml or 80 ml
Meat stock	500 ml	1 litre	2 litres
Cake flour	50 ml (25 g)	100 ml (50 g)	300 ml (150 g)
Buttermilk pastry:			
Self-raising flour	250 ml (120 g)	450 ml (225 g)	850 ml (400 g)
Salt	1 ml	3 ml	5 ml
Butter	60 g	125 g	250 g
Buttermilk	80 ml	125 ml	250 ml
Eggs	1	2	4
Milk	20 ml	30 ml	60 ml

Preparation
☐ Cube the meat.
☐ Peel and chop the onions finely.
☐ Peel and crush the garlic cloves.

Method
Brown the meat in heated oil in a heavy-based saucepan. Add the onions and garlic and sauté until the onions are translucent. Add the seasonings and heated stock. Cover with the lid, reduce the heat and simmer for 2-2½ hours or until the meat is tender. Thicken the gravy with the flour mixed to a paste with water.

Prepare the buttermilk pastry: Sift the dry ingredients together. Rub in the butter with your fingertips. Beat the buttermilk, eggs and milk together and mix with the dry ingredients to make a soft pastry. Chill for 1 hour and roll out to 5 mm thick.

Spoon the meat into an ovenproof dish and cover with the pastry. Brush with beaten egg and bake for 20 minutes at 200 °C (400 °F) or until golden brown.

Tips
☐ Beef shin can be replaced by boned lamb neck or shin. Season lamb with rosemary rather than mixed herbs.
☐ Prepare the beef pie in individual portions and freeze before baking the pastry.

Gingered sweet potatoes

(12 servings; use 2 or 4 times the quantities for 24 or 48 servings)

2,1 kg medium sweet potatoes, cut into 20 mm thick slices
150 ml ginger syrup
50 ml ginger pieces
2 ml ground ginger
10 ml lemon juice
5 ml salt
100 ml butter

Method
Layer the sweet potatoes in an ovenproof dish. Add the syrup, ginger pieces, ground ginger, lemon juice and salt. Dot with butter, cover and bake for 30 minutes at 180 °C (350 °F). Remove the covering and bake for a further 10-15 minutes at 200 °C (400 °F) until glazed.

Menu

Potbread* with green figs

Beef pie with buttermilk pastry*
Gingered sweet potatoes*
Buttered mixed vegetables
Onion salad with sour sauce*

Cinnamon dumplings*
with custard

For 12 people you will need:
☐ 12 green figs in syrup
☐ 1,2 kg mixed vegetables
☐ 600 ml custard

Pineapple-glazed ham

Ingredients	12 servings	24 servings	48 servings
Mustard powder	10 ml	20 ml	40 ml
White pepper	2 ml	3 ml	5 ml
Pickled leg of pork	2,4 kg	4,8 kg	9,6 kg
Pineapple glaze:			
Canned pineapple pieces, puréed	½ x 410 g	1 x 410 g	2 x 410 g
Apricot jam	60 ml	100 ml	200 ml
Whole ginger preserve	30 ml	60 ml	100 ml

Preparation

☐ Purée the pineapple pieces.

Method

Rub the mustard powder and pepper over the pork. Place on aluminium foil and cover. Bake for 40 minutes per 500 g in a preheated oven at 160 °C (325 °F). Remove from the oven and remove the rind. Mix the ingredients for the pineapple glaze. Place the ham on the rack of a roasting pan and roast for 20-30 minutes at 180 °C (350 °F), brushing often with the glaze. Serve hot or cold.

Tips

☐ If pineapple pieces are not available, glaze the ham with melted youngberry jam, green fig preserve or honey and lemon juice. If desired, add 5 ml ground ginger and 15 ml lemon juice to the basting mixture.

☐ The same method is followed if the ham is both pickled and smoked.

Menu

Smoked trout fillets in an orange marinade*

Pineapple-glazed ham*
Potato salad with bacon
Poached yellow plums*
Copper penny salad*
Marinated broccoli and red sweet peppers*

Cheesecake with gooseberries*

For 12 people you will need:

☐ potato salad:
1,8 kg potatoes
360 ml sour cream
100 ml chopped spring onions
250 g bacon, crisply fried

Above from left: Copper penny salad (p. 80); Potato salad with bacon (menu); Cheesecake with gooseberries (p. 80) and Marinated broccoli and red sweet peppers (p. 90). Front: Pineapple-glazed ham.

Smoked trout fillets in an orange marinade

(12 servings; use 2 or 4 times the quantities for 24 or 48 servings)

350 ml fresh orange juice
5 ml grated lemon peel
15 ml chopped fresh dill or fennel
12 smoked trout fillets (60 g each), sliced paper-thin
segments of 2 oranges
fresh herbs for garnishing

Method
Mix the orange juice, lemon peel and dill in a glass dish. Marinate the trout fillets for 3 hours in the marinade. Garnish with orange segments and fresh herbs.

Tip
☐ Smoked salmon may be used instead of trout.

Poached yellow plums

(12 servings; use 2 or 4 times the quantities for 24 or 48 servings)

250 ml sugar
250 ml water
peel of 1 orange
15 ml lemon juice
1,5 kg yellow plums
30 ml Cointreau

Method
Dissolve the sugar in the water over low heat. Add the peel and juice and simmer for 5 minutes. Place the plums in the boiling syrup, remove from the stove immediately (otherwise the plums will get too soft) and add the Cointreau. Cool. Serve chilled.

Copper penny salad

(12 servings; use 2 or 4 times the quantities for 24 or 48 servings, but 1½ or 3 times the quantity of vinegar)

1,2 kg carrots, sliced
10 spring onions, finely chopped
250 ml tomato purée
200 ml wine vinegar
50 ml cooking oil
10 ml Worcester sauce
250 ml sugar
5 ml prepared mustard
5 ml salt
freshly ground black pepper to taste

Method
Boil the carrots until tender but still firm. Place in a salad dish with the spring onions. Heat the remaining ingredients to boiling point, allow to cool and pour over the carrots. Marinate for 1-2 days in the refrigerator.

Cheesecake with gooseberries

(12 servings; use 2 or 4 times the quantities for 24 or 48 servings, and make in separate containers)

Base
1 packet (200 g) Tennis biscuits, crushed
50 ml toasted coconut
120 ml melted butter

Filling
250 ml milk
200 g castor sugar
4 egg yolks
30 g gelatine
50 ml water
500 ml cream, stiffly whipped
500 g cream cheese
10 ml lemon juice
10 ml lemon peel
canned gooseberries for garnishing
icing sugar for garnishing

Method
Prepare the base by mixing the Tennis biscuits, coconut and butter. Press into a loose-based 225 mm pan.

Prepare the filling: Beat the milk, castor sugar and egg yolks together and heat in a double boiler to make a custard. Soak the gelatine in the water and heat slightly until dissolved. Allow to cool and add to the custard mixture.

Add the whipped cream, cream cheese, lemon juice and peel to the custard mixture and mix. Pour into the base. Cool and decorate with gooseberries. Sprinkle a little icing sugar over and serve.

Tip
☐ The gooseberries can be thickened with 25 ml custard powder and poured over the filling. Allow to set.

Kassler rib with apricot glaze

Ingredients	12 servings	24 servings	48 servings
Kassler rib	3 kg (12 ribs)	5,5 kg (24 ribs)	10,5 kg (48 ribs)
Ginger ale	70 ml	125 ml	250 ml
Apricot glaze:			
Canned apricot halves, puréed	1 x 410 g	2 x 410 g	3 x 410 g
Lemon peel	5 ml	10 ml	20 ml
Lemon juice	10 ml	20 ml	40 ml
Apricot jam	70 ml	150 ml	250 ml
Brown sugar	10 ml	15 ml	30 ml

Preparation

☐ Mix all the glaze ingredients in a small saucepan and heat to boiling point. Allow to cool.

Method

Sprinkle the meat with ginger ale. Cover the meat with aluminium foil (shiny side in) and bake for 2 hours in a preheated oven at 160 °C (325 °F), or until meat is cooked. Place the meat on the rack of a roasting pan, fat side up. Roast for 30-40 minutes at 180 °C (350 °F), basting constantly with the glaze. Serve cold or hot.

Tips

☐ Ask your butcher to saw through the bones of the Kassler rib to make carving easier.

☐ A Kassler rib usually consists of 8 ribs and is thus sufficient for 8 servings.

Crudités with dips

Crudités can be described as cut fresh vegetables served with a variety of dips. Different vegetables are cut into bite-sized pieces, creating a feast of colour, texture and shape. Choose fresh, crisp vegetables and arrange them on trays or a flat serving dish to contrast colours and shapes, e.g. young carrots or carrot strips (julienne carrots), celery stalks, blanched young green beans, whole cherry tomatoes and broccoli florets. Choose seasonal vegetables to ensure the best quality. For 12 people you will need:

6 carrots, cut into julienne strips
200 g mangetout
6 celery stalks, cut into bite-sized pieces
200 g young mealies
24 cherry tomatoes
300 g broccoli and cauliflower florets

Cucumber sour cream dip

(48 servings; use ¼ or ½ of the quantities for 12 or 24 servings)

2 English cucumbers, peeled, seeded and finely grated
1 garlic clove, finely chopped
500 ml sour cream or smooth low-fat cottage cheese
125 ml chopped fresh parsley (or other fresh herbs)
salt and white pepper to taste

Method

Combine all the ingredients and chill. Serve with crudités (also see dips on p. 92).

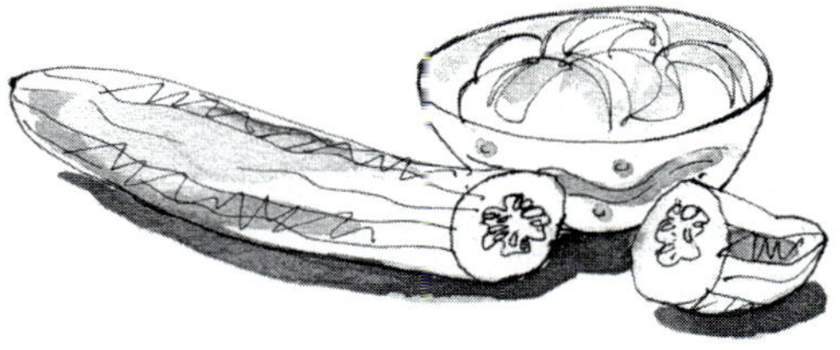

Menu

Crudités* with dips*

Kassler rib with apricot glaze*
Lemony new potatoes*
Mixed green vegetables
Citrus salad with celery*

White chocolate mousse*

For 12 people you will need:

☐ 1,2 kg green vegetables

Stuffed whole chicken

Ingredients	12 servings	24 servings	48 servings
Whole chickens	2	6	8
Salt	10 ml	20 ml	40 ml
White pepper	4 ml	8 ml	15 ml
Ham and mushroom stuffing:			
Medium onions, chopped	100 g (1)	200 g (2)	400 g (4)
Butter	15 ml	25 ml	50 ml
Brown mushrooms, chopped	250 g	500 g	1 kg
Ham, chopped	125 g	250 g	500 g
Fresh breadcrumbs	100 ml	200 ml	350 ml
Salt	5 ml	10 ml	20 ml
Freshly ground black pepper	2 ml	4 ml	7 ml
Celery and nut stuffing:			
Small onion, chopped	100 g (1)	200 g (2)	400 g (4)
Butter, melted	50 g	100 g	200 g
Celery stalks, chopped	4	7	12
Dried apricots, soaked and coarsely chopped	70 g	150 g	300 g
Pecan nuts, coarsely chopped	50 g	100 g	200 g
Fresh breadcrumbs	100 ml	200 ml	400 ml
Chopped fresh parsley	15 ml	30 ml	50 ml
Salt	5 ml	10 ml	20 ml
Freshly ground black pepper	2 ml	4 ml	8 ml
Brown rice stuffing:			
Bacon, chopped	100 g	200 g	400 g
Medium onions, chopped	100 g (1)	200 g (2)	400 g (4)
Celery stalks, chopped	3	6	12
Butter	15 ml	30 ml	50 ml
Brown rice, cooked	250 ml	2 x 250 ml	4 x 250 ml
Salt	5 ml	10 ml	20 ml
Freshly ground black pepper	2 ml	4 ml	8 ml
Dried or chopped fresh mixed herbs	5 ml or 15 ml	10 ml or 30 ml	20 ml or 60 ml
Chopped fresh parsley	10 ml	20 ml	40 ml

Preparation

☐ Prepare the chickens: Remove the giblets and wipe the chicken with paper towels. Clean the breast cavity. Stuff the neck cavity with the stuffing of your choice, fold the skin of the neck back and secure it with a skewer. Now stuff the body cavity, close and secure with skewers. Press the drumsticks close to the body and insert a long skewer through the middle joints to secure them to the body. Cross the lower joints and tie to the tail with string. Press the wings close to the body and insert a long skewer through both. With the breast side up, hook string around each skewer and tie it securely. Season the chicken with salt and pepper. Place it in a cooking bag, secure and bake at 180 °C (350 °F) for 1-1½

Menu

Mini lamb kebabs with mint sauce*

Stuffed whole chicken*
Roast potatoes
Pumpkin with ginger syrup*
Buttered green beans
Crisp green salad with pineapple

Baked brown pudding with caramel custard*

For 12 people you will need:

☐ 2,1 kg (12 medium) potatoes
☐ 1,2 kg green beans
☐ salad ingredients:
1 large butter lettuce
1 medium onion
2 medium green sweet peppers
3 medium green apples
200 g mangetout
1 medium pineapple

hours or until golden brown. Remove the skewers and string and serve immediately.

- ☐ Prepare the stuffing(s):
  prepare the vegetables, nuts and herbs;
  prepare the meat;
  cook the rice.

Method

Ham and Mushroom Stuffing
Sauté the onion in heated butter until translucent. Add the mushrooms and fry for a few minutes. Mix with the remaining ingredients, divide into equal quantities and use as a stuffing for chicken.

Celery and Nut Stuffing
Sauté the onion in heated butter until translucent. Add the celery and fry for a few minutes. Add the remaining ingredients, mix lightly and divide into equal quantities. Use as a stuffing for chicken.

Brown Rice Stuffing
Fry the bacon until crisp. Add the onion and sauté until translucent. Add the celery and butter and fry for a further 2 minutes. Add the remaining ingredients and mix lightly. Divide into equal quantities and use as a stuffing for chicken.

Mini lamb kebabs with mint sauce

(48 servings; use ¼ or ½ of the quantities for 12 or 24 servings)

150 ml olive or cooking oil
60 ml lemon juice
salt and freshly ground black pepper to taste
5 ml dried or 15 ml chopped fresh mint
10 ml grated lemon peel
2,4 kg boned leg of lamb or thick rib of lamb, cut into strips
96 bamboo skewers

Mint Sauce
60 ml water
30 ml castor sugar
80 ml chopped fresh mint
125 ml white wine vinegar

Method

Mix the oil, lemon juice, seasonings, mint and lemon peel thoroughly in a glass dish and marinate the meat in the mixture for 3 hours. Drain the meat and thread it concertina-wise onto the skewers. Place the kebabs 100 mm below the oven grilling element and grill for 15 minutes or until cooked. Keep warm.

Prepare the mint sauce: Heat the water and sugar to boiling point, allow to cool and add the mint and vinegar. Serve immediately with the lamb kebabs.

Tips

- ☐ Prepare the mint sauce a few hours beforehand.
- ☐ Soak the bamboo skewers in water for 30 minutes before threading the meat onto them, so that they don't scorch during grilling.

Baked brown pudding with caramel custard

(12 servings; use 2 or 4 times the quantities for 24 or 48 servings and mix batter in 2 or 4 separate containers for best results)

Batter
5 ml bicarbonate of soda
125 ml milk
375 ml (180 g) self-raising flour
125 ml white sugar
2 eggs
40 ml apricot jam
25 ml soft butter
1 ml salt
5 ml ground ginger

Sauce
250 ml water
250 ml cream
125 ml butter
125 ml sugar
5 ml vanilla essence

Caramel Custard
600 ml custard
5 ml caramel essence

Method

Prepare the batter by dissolving the bicarbonate of soda in the milk. Sift the flour and add to the milk with the remaining ingredients. Mix to a smooth batter. Pour into a 2-litre ovenproof dish. Bake for 30 minutes at 180 °C (350 °F) or until cooked.

Heat all the sauce ingredients to boiling point. Pour the hot sauce over the pudding as soon as it comes from the oven.

Flavour the custard mixture with caramel essence. Serve the pudding with caramel-flavoured custard.

Oven-roasted pepper Scotch fillet

Ingredients	12 servings	24 servings	48 servings
Scotch fillet	2 kg	4 kg	7,5 kg
Lemon juice	20 ml	35 ml	75 ml
Salt	10 ml	20 ml	40 ml
Butter, melted	60 g	100 g	200 g
Coarsely ground black pepper	about 150 ml	about 250 ml	about 500 ml

Preparation

☐ Carefully remove the outer fat layer from the meat. Sprinkle the lemon juice over the meat, season with salt and brush with melted butter. Sprinkle the black pepper onto a wooden board and roll the meat over the pepper until the surface is covered with pepper. Allow the meat to rest in the refrigerator for 30-45 minutes.

Method

Place the meat on the rack of a roasting pan and roast at 160 °C (325 °F): 15-20 minutes per 500 g plus 15 minutes extra for rare; 20-25 minutes per 500 g plus 20 minutes extra for medium. Allow the meat to rest in a warming drawer for 10 minutes to facilitate carving. Carve the meat thinly. Serve hot or cold.

Mock pesto sauce

(48 servings; use ¼ or ½ of the quantities for 12 or 24 servings)

100 g parsley
6 garlic cloves, crushed
200 g walnuts or almonds
150 ml olive oil
70 ml water
150 g grated Parmesan cheese
120 ml chopped fresh basil
120 g soft butter
10 ml salt
5 ml freshly ground black pepper

Method

Place all the ingredients in a food processor and mix until smooth. Serve with the peppered Scotch fillet.

Tip

☐ Pesto sauce can be stored for up to 3 weeks in the refrigerator.

Menu

Pâté with rye bread

Oven-roasted pepper Scotch fillet*
Mock pesto sauce*
Parsley new potatoes
Creamed spinach
Aniseed carrots*
Fresh green salad

Cheese and biscuits
Fresh fruit

For 12 people you will need:

☐ 600 ml pâté
☐ 2 small rye loaves (24 slices)
☐ 1,3 kg new potatoes
☐ 1,5 kg spinach (tough stalks removed)
☐ 250 ml cream
☐ salad ingredients:
1 large butter lettuce
100 g watercress
200 g bean sprouts
200 g mushrooms
450 g baby marrows
☐ 3-4 (300 g each) cheeses of your choice
☐ 36 (3 kinds x 12 each) savoury biscuits
☐ fresh fruit:
1,8 kg grapes (green and black)
8-12 peaches

Oven-roasted loin of pork with orange

Ingredients	12 servings	24 servings	48 servings
Boned loin of pork, rind and excess fat removed	2 kg	2 x 2 kg	4 x 2 kg
Lemon juice	20 ml	40 ml	80 ml
Garlic cloves, crushed	2	4	8
Dried or chopped fresh rosemary	5 ml or 15 ml	10 ml or 30 ml	20 ml or 60 ml
Salt	7 ml	15 ml	20 ml
Freshly ground black pepper	3 ml	5 ml	10 ml
Orange basting sauce:			
Peel of oranges	2	4	8
Fresh orange juice	60 ml	125 ml	250 ml
French mustard	15 ml	25 ml	40 ml
Marmalade or apricot jam	50 ml	80 ml	150 ml
Brown sugar	15 ml	30 ml	60 ml
Orange liqueur (optional)	25 ml	40 ml	80 ml

Preparation

☐ Prepare the meat by sprinkling the lemon juice, garlic, rosemary and half the salt and pepper on the inside. Roll up the meat and secure at 25 mm intervals with string.

☐ Place all the ingredients for the orange basting sauce in a saucepan and heat to boiling point.

Method

Season the meat with the remaining salt and pepper. Place the meat on the rack of an oven-roasting pan and oven-roast at 160 °C (325 °F) for 25-30 minutes per 500 g plus 25 minutes extra. Baste the meat with the basting sauce for the last 30-40 minutes or until the meat is golden brown. Allow the meat to rest for 10 minutes in the warming drawer to facilitate carving. Remove the string and carve thinly.

Hollandaise sauce

(12 servings; use 2 or 4 times the quantities for 24 or 48 servings)

4 egg yolks
350 g butter, cubed
6 ml lemon juice
salt and white pepper to taste
chopped fresh parsley (optional)
250 ml sour cream

Method

Place the egg yolks in a double boiler, beating constantly. Add the butter cubes gradually, beating constantly. Continue beating until thick and cooked. Season with the lemon juice, seasoning and parsley. Allow to cool, then add the sour cream.

Menu

Turban of sole* with hollandaise sauce*

Oven-roasted loin of pork with orange*
Gingered sweet potatoes*
Buttered young vegetables
Green salad with fresh herbs

Crème caramel*

For 12 people you will need:

☐ young vegetables:
300 g patty pans
300 g young mealies
350 g young carrots
200 g pickling onions

☐ salad ingredients:
300 g lettuce, various kinds
36 cherry tomatoes
4 medium carrots
150 g cheese cubes
125 ml chopped fresh herbs

Butterflied leg of lamb with caper butter topping

Ingredients	12 servings	24 servings	48 servings
Boned leg of lamb	2 kg	3,6 kg	3 x 2,4 kg
Salt	10 ml	17 ml	30 ml
Freshly ground black pepper	3 ml	5 ml	10 ml
Caper butter topping:			
Soft butter	80 ml	150 ml	300 ml
Cooking oil	10 ml	15 ml	30 ml
Lemon juice	20 ml	40 ml	80 ml
Garlic cloves, crushed	2	4	8
Dijon mustard	15 ml	25 ml	50 ml
Capers, chopped	15 ml	25 ml	45 ml
Salt	3 ml	5 ml	10 ml
Freshly ground black pepper	2 ml	3 ml	5 ml

Preparation

☐ Open out the boned leg of lamb and flatten the meat evenly with a meat mallet or the palm of your hand.

☐ Make diamond-shaped incisions in the fat layer. Season with salt and pepper.

☐ Mix the butter, oil, lemon juice, garlic, mustard, capers, salt and pepper thoroughly and spread it over the meat. Chill for 1 hour.

Method

Place the meat on the rack of an oven-roasting pan and oven-roast at 160 °C (325 °F): 20-25 minutes per 500 g plus 20 minutes extra for medium; 25-30 minutes per 500 g plus 25 minutes extra for well done.

Leave the meat in a warming drawer for 10 minutes to facilitate carving. Carve the meat thinly and serve hot or cold.

Tip

☐ Instead of leg of lamb, you can use a butterflied shoulder of lamb (2 kg; 2 x 1,8 kg; 5 x 1,5 kg).

Salmon with lemon dill sauce

(12 servings; use 2 or 4 times the quantities for 24 or 48 servings)

12 x 60 g salmon (cut 5 mm thick)
grated lemon peel for garnishing

LEMON DILL SAUCE
250 ml sour cream
15 ml lemon juice
10 ml grated lemon peel
salt and pepper to taste
5 ml dried or 15 ml chopped fresh dill

Method

Prepare the lemon dill sauce by mixing all the ingredients together thoroughly and then cooling them. Pour the sauce onto individual hors d'oeuvres plates and tilt the plates to spread the sauce evenly. Arrange the salmon, concertina-wise, on top of the sauce and garnish with the chopped peel.

Menu

Salmon with lemon dill sauce*

Butterflied leg of lamb with caper butter topping*
Mashed potato and leek rosettes*
Young beets with youngberry sauce*
Roasted leeks*
Butter lettuce salad with croutons*

Pancake nests with fresh fruit*

For 12 people you will need:

☐ salad ingredients:
1 large butter lettuce
200 g fresh young green beans
24 green olives
240 g mangetout
24 yellow cherry tomatoes
croutons made from 4 slices white bread

Additional recipes

STARTERS

Turban of sole

(12 servings; use 2 or 4 times the quantities for 24 or 48 servings)

6 soles, each cut into 4 fillets
180 ml fish or chicken stock
5 ml dried or 15 ml chopped fresh dill
5 ml dried or 15 ml chopped fresh parsley
juice of 3 lemons
salt and white pepper to taste

Method
Roll up each fish fillet and secure it with a cocktail stick. Mix the stock, herbs and lemon juice. Pack the fish fillets in an ovenproof dish, pour the lemon sauce over, season with salt and pepper and bake for 30-40 minutes at 180 °C (350 °F) or until fish is cooked. Drain and serve with hollandaise sauce.

Marinated salmon trout

(12 servings; use 2 or 4 times the quantities for 24 or 48 servings)

12 x 60 g smoked salmon trout
fresh herbs and lemon wedges for garnishing

Garlic Marinade
30 ml wine vinegar
30 ml lemon juice
1 ml salt
5 ml French mustard
freshly ground black pepper to taste
50 ml olive or salad oil
15 ml sugar
2 garlic cloves, crushed
30 ml chopped parsley

Method
Prepare the garlic marinade: Place all the ingredients in a glass or ceramic container and mix thoroughly. Refrigerate for 2 hours to allow the flavours to develop.

Place the salmon trout in a glass or ceramic container and pour the marinade over. Marinate for 2-4 hours in the refrigerator. Drain and serve with fresh herbs and a lemon wedge.

Marinated biltong on watercress

(12 servings; use 2 or 4 times the quantities for 24 or 48 servings)

12 x 40 g sliced beef biltong
200 g watercress
fresh dill sprig for garnishing

Marinade
30 ml lemon juice
30 ml wine vinegar
30 ml mayonnaise
5 ml prepared mustard
1 ml cayenne pepper
5 ml dried or 15 ml chopped fresh basil
10 ml sugar

Method
Prepare the marinade: Mix the ingredients thoroughly and leave to stand overnight.

Place the biltong in a glass or ceramic container and pour the marinade over. Marinate for 1 hour. Drain and serve with watercress, garnished with a fresh dill sprig.

Mushroom quiche

(6 very large or 8 servings; use 2, 3 or 6 times the quantities for 12, 24 or 48 servings and make individual quiches)

100 ml chopped chives
250 g mushrooms, sliced
50 ml butter
1 savoury pastry case
250 ml sour cream
3 eggs, beaten
salt and white pepper to taste
20 ml chopped fresh dill or fennel
200 ml grated Cheddar cheese

Method
Sauté the chives and mushrooms in butter until cooked. Allow to cool slightly and spoon into the base of the pastry case. Beat the sour cream, eggs, seasonings and dill together thoroughly and pour over the mushroom mixture. Sprinkle the cheese on top and bake for 45 minutes at 180 °C (350 °F) or until the egg mixture has set.

Chicken-filled phyllo parcels

(48 servings; use ¼ or ½ of the quantities for 12 or 24 servings)

2-5 cooked chicken breasts, chilled
15 ml butter
30 ml (15 g) cake flour
5 ml mild curry powder
250 ml milk or cream
2 ml nutmeg
salt and white pepper to taste
250 g butter
50 sheets phyllo pastry

Method
Remove the skin from the chicken and cut the flesh into small pieces. Melt the butter in a small saucepan. Add the flour and curry powder and cook for a few minutes over low heat. Add the milk, stirring constantly. Cook over low heat until the sauce thickens. Add the seasonings and chicken. Cool. Melt the butter. Cut the phyllo sheets into 10 cm x 30 cm strips. Brush the strips with melted butter. Spoon a teaspoonful of chicken mixture onto the end of each strip and fold up the pastry at right angles to make triangles. Continue folding until you reach the end of the strip. Place on a baking sheet and bake in a preheated oven at 200 °C (400 °F) until golden brown.

Variation

Phyllo parcels with spinach

(48 servings; use ¼ or ½ of the quantities for 12 or 24 servings)

200 g frozen spinach, drained
1 small onion
10 ml butter
50 ml dried breadcrumbs
salt and pepper to taste

Method
Drain the spinach thoroughly. Sauté the onion in the butter and add the spinach. Reduce the heat and simmer until reduced. Add the breadcrumbs and season. Cool. Continue preparing the phyllo parcels as described in the previous recipe.

Tips
☐ Cover the phyllo pastry with a damp cloth while making the parcels, to prevent its drying out.
☐ These phyllo parcels can be frozen for up to 2 weeks.

Mock chicken drumsticks peri-peri

(24 servings; use ½ or 2 times the quantities for 12 or 48 servings)

50 chicken wings
350 ml melted butter
100 ml lemon juice
50 ml peri-peri
salt and freshly ground black pepper to taste

Method
Snip the wing tip and centre joint of each chicken wing with a boning knife, loosen the meat around the joint, move the meat carefully down the bone and turn the meat on the inside to the outside. Brush the wings with the butter. Sprinkle with lemon juice, followed by peri-peri, salt and pepper. Place on a baking sheet and bake for 30-45 minutes in a preheated oven at 180 °C (350 °F) or until cooked. Brush with melted butter, if necessary. Serve hot or cold.

Tip
☐ As a variation, use 150 ml freshly chopped or 50 ml dried mixed herbs instead of the peri-peri.

Tomato and mozzarella salad with fresh basil

(12 servings; use 2 or 4 times the quantities for 24 or 48 servings)

6 large, ripe tomatoes, sliced
600 g mozzarella cheese, cut into 5 mm thick slices
24 basil leaves, chopped
60 ml olive oil
30 ml lemon juice
salt and freshly ground black pepper to taste

Method
Arrange the tomatoes and cheese on a flat salad dish. Sprinkle basil over. Mix the olive oil and lemon juice and sprinkle over the salad. Season with salt and pepper.

SALAD

Citrus salad with celery

(12 servings; use 2 or 4 times the quantities for 24 or 48 servings)

12 oranges, segmented
6 grapefruit, segmented
1 can (210 g) nectarines, drained
2 green apples, cut into wedges
4 celery stalks, sliced diagonally
50 ml sultanas (optional)
15 ml chopped fresh mint for garnishing

Method
Mix ingredients and chill. Garnish with mint.

Potato salad

(12 servings; use 2 or 4 times the quantities for 24 or 48 servings)

12 (about 2 kg) cooked medium potatoes, sliced
2 onions, finely chopped
10 gherkins, finely chopped
4 hard-boiled eggs, chopped
chives for garnishing

Method
Arrange the potato slices on a flat salad dish. Sprinkle the onions, gherkins and eggs over. Pour a sauce of your choice over and garnish.

Choice 1: Mustard Mayonnaise
150 ml mayonnaise
50 ml natural yoghurt
10 ml Pommery mustard
15 ml lemon juice
2 ml salt

Choice 2: Blaauwkrantz Cheese Sauce
250 ml sour cream
15 ml lemon juice
5 ml lemon peel
salt and freshly ground black pepper to taste
100 g Blaauwkrantz cheese, grated

Method
Mix all the ingredients thoroughly and chill.

Tips
☐ Sprinkle crisply fried bacon over the salad.
☐ Crisp croutons can be sprinkled over the salad just before serving.
☐ For an interesting variation, add chopped fresh herbs to the mustard mayonnaise.
☐ Chopped walnuts or toasted almonds make a deliciously crunchy addition to potato salad.

Coleslaw with yoghurt dressing

(12 servings; use 2 or 4 times the quantities for 24 or 48 servings)

1 cabbage, finely shredded
125 ml sultanas or seedless raisins
½ pineapple, cubed
2 carrots, grated

Yoghurt Dressing
300 ml natural yoghurt or cream
30 ml honey
30 ml lemon juice
15 ml lemon peel
20 ml chopped ginger root

Method
Prepare the yoghurt dressing by mixing all the ingredients and chilling it for 2 hours. Mix the salad ingredients thoroughly, pour the yoghurt dressing over and chill.

Onion salad with sour sauce

(12 servings; use 2 or 4 times the quantities for 24 or 48 servings, but 1½ or 3 times the quantity of vinegar)

1,2 kg pickling onions, peeled
chopped fresh dill or fennel for garnishing

Sour Sauce
2 eggs
50 ml sugar
2 ml salt
5 ml cornflour
50 ml vinegar
60 ml water
100 ml sour cream

Method
Cut a cross in the root end of each onion and boil them for about 30-40 minutes or until tender. Drain.

Prepare the sour sauce: Beat the eggs thoroughly. Add the rest of the ingredients, except the sour cream, and beat well. Place the mixture in a double boiler and heat until the sauce thickens. Beat constantly to prevent the sauce from curdling. Allow to cool, then add the sour cream. Mix thoroughly and pour the sauce over the onions. Garnish with chopped fresh dill or fennel.

Hot potato salad with Blaauwkrantz cheese sauce

(24 servings; use ½ or 2 times the quantities for 12 or 48 servings)

25 medium potatoes
500 g bacon, cubed
2 bunches chives, chopped
freshly ground black pepper
bunch of fresh herbs for garnishing

Blaauwkrantz Cheese Sauce
250 g Blaauwkrantz cheese, grated
500 ml cream
250 ml natural yoghurt
25 ml lemon juice
salt and freshly ground black pepper to taste

Method
Boil the potatoes until tender, peel and slice them. Arrange the hot potatoes in a serving dish. Keep warm. Fry the bacon until crisp. Prepare the cheese sauce: Mix all the ingredients thoroughly. Pour the sauce over the potatoes. Sprinkle chives and bacon over and season with black pepper. Garnish with a bunch of fresh herbs

Green salad with cottage cheese and nuts

(12 large servings; use 2 or 4 times the quantities for 24 or 48 servings)

2 heads of lettuce, broken into bite-sized pieces
2 red sweet peppers, cubed
500 g chunky cottage cheese
350 ml yoghurt
30 ml mayonnaise
30 ml honey
200 g chopped nuts

Method
Arrange the lettuce on a salad dish. Sprinkle sweet pepper cubes over. Spoon the cottage cheese on top. Mix the yoghurt, mayonnaise and honey and pour the mixture over the cottage cheese. Sprinkle the nuts over and serve immediately.

Crushed wheat salad

(12 servings; use 2 or 4 times the quantities for 24 or 48 servings)

500 ml crushed wheat
2 onions, finely chopped
6 large gherkins, finely chopped
100 g chopped nuts
1 can (410 g) peach halves
50 g raisins
1 green sweet pepper, cubed
250 ml home-made mayonnaise
10 ml French mustard

Method
Boil the wheat until done. Allow to cool slightly and mix with the remaining ingredients. Chill.

SIDE DISHES

Marinated broccoli and red sweet peppers

(12 servings; use 2 or 4 times the quantities for 24 or 48 servings)

900 g broccoli florets
2 red sweet peppers, cut into julienne strips

MARINADE
125 ml olive or salad oil
5 ml salt
2 ml freshly ground black pepper
5 ml each dried parsley, basil and oregano
60 ml wine vinegar
15 ml sugar
40 ml mayonnaise
4 cloves garlic, crushed

Method
Prepare the marinade by mixing all the ingredients thoroughly and chilling them overnight. Pour the marinade over the broccoli and sweet peppers and marinate them for 2-4 hours. Drain and serve chilled.

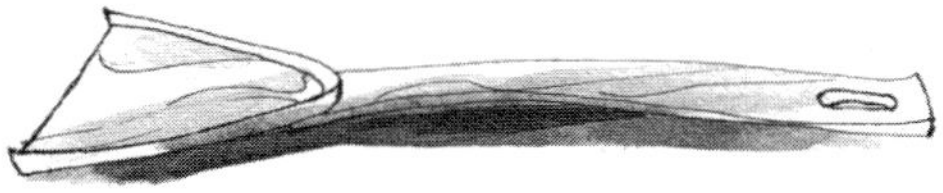

Ratatouille with sweet peppers

(12 servings; use 2 or 4 times the quantities for 24 or 48 servings)

2 medium onions, cut into rings
1 garlic clove, crushed
15 ml butter
1 green sweet pepper, cut into julienne strips
2 red sweet peppers, cut into julienne strips
1 young medium brinjal, cubed
8 baby marrows, cut into rounds
3 large ripe tomatoes, skinned and puréed
salt and freshly ground black pepper to taste
150 ml white meat stock or white wine

Method
Sauté the onions and garlic in butter until translucent. Add the sweet peppers, brinjal and baby marrows and fry for a few minutes. Add the tomatoes, seasonings and heated liquid. Cover and simmer for 15-20 minutes.

Fried rice

(12 servings; use 2 or 4 times the quantities for 24 or 48 servings)

60 ml butter
125 ml finely chopped chives
1,5 litres cooked rice (500 g uncooked)
5 ml soy sauce (optional)

Method
Heat the butter in a large pan. Add the chives and sauté. Add the cooked rice and fry it lightly. Add the optional soy sauce and stir it in.

Roasted leeks

(12 servings; use 2 or 4 times the quantities for 24 or 48 servings)

1,1 kg leeks, green leaves removed, halved lengthways
4 garlic cloves, crushed
60 ml butter
30 ml olive oil
20 ml lemon juice
40 g Parmesan cheese
100 ml dried breadcrumbs

Method
Pack the leeks in a single layer in an ovenproof dish. Place the garlic, butter, oil and lemon juice in a small saucepan and heat slightly. Pour over the leeks. Cover and bake for 20-25 minutes at 180 °C (350 °F) or until tender. Sprinkle the Parmesan cheese and breadcrumbs over and bake at 200 °C (400 °F) until golden brown.

Oven-baked pickling onions

(24 servings; use ½ or 2 times the quantities for 12 or 48 servings)

100 pickling onions or young onions
10 ml salt
500 g butter
white pepper to taste
3 x 40 g grated Parmesan cheese
chopped oregano or parsley for garnishing

Method
Blanch the onions in boiling water and salt for 2 minutes. Peel while still hot and cut a cross in the root end of each onion. Pack the onions in a single layer in a roasting pan, dot with butter, sprinkle pepper over, cover with aluminium foil and bake for 30 minutes at 180 °C (350 °F) or until the onions are tender. Sprinkle the Parmesan cheese over and bake for 10 minutes at 200 °C (400 °F) until lightly coloured. Garnish with chopped oregano or parsley.

Orange carrots

(12 servings; use 2 or 4 times the quantities for 24 and 48 servings)

1,4 kg carrots, sliced diagonally
2 ml salt
500 ml fresh orange juice
10 ml grated orange peel
25 ml brown sugar
25 ml butter

Place all the ingredients in a saucepan and cook until the carrots are tender but still crisp. Drain and serve.

Variation
Aniseed carrots: Add 5 ml aniseed to the ingredients and follow the method given above.

Young beets with youngberry sauce

(12 servings; use 2 or 4 times the quantities for 24 or 48 servings)

1,2 kg young beets with 3 cm of the stalks
500 ml youngberry juice
15 ml chopped fresh fennel
1 ml salt
15 ml cornflour

Method
Boil the young beets for 30-45 minutes in the youngberry juice, or until tender. Remove the skins, add the fennel and salt and thicken the sauce with the cornflour mixed to a paste with water.

Mashed potato and leek rosettes

(12 servings; use 2 or 4 times the quantities for 24 or 48 servings)

8 leeks, cut into rings
10 ml butter
10 large cooked potatoes, mashed
2 ml nutmeg
2 eggs, beaten
salt and pepper to taste
200 ml grated Cheddar cheese (optional)

Method
Sauté the leeks in heated butter until soft and transparent. Purée them and add to the mashed potatoes with the nutmeg, eggs, salt, pepper and cheese. Mix well. Place the potato mixture in a piping bag and pipe rosettes on a greased baking sheet. Bake in a preheated oven at 200 °C (400 °F) until lightly browned. Remove carefully from the baking sheet – they break easily.

BREAD

Olive bread

(2 loaves/24 servings, about 40 thin slices; use ½ or 2 times the quantities for 12 or 48 servings (1 or 4 loaves) and make in separate containers)

24 black olives, stoned and halved
20 ml chopped fresh rosemary
2 kg white bread dough
coarse salt

Method
Add the olives and rosemary to the bread dough and knead thoroughly. Place in a loaf pan and allow to rise. Sprinkle the coarse salt over and bake for 45-60 minutes at 180 °C (350 °F).

Tips
☐ White bread dough is freely available from supermarkets and bakeries, or use the Potbread recipe on p. 92.
☐ A little olive oil can be brushed over the surface of the dough to add extra flavour.

Potbread (Ronel Joubert)

(2 loaves, 24 servings, about 25 large slices: use ½ or 2 times the quantities for 12 or 48 servings [1 or 4 loaves])

10 g instant yeast
1 kg white bread flour
10 ml sugar
15 ml salt
75 g butter
650 ml lukewarm water

Method
Sift the dry ingredients together and rub in the butter. Add the water and mix thoroughly. Allow to rise. Knock down and place in two greased loaf pans. Leave for 1 hour to rise. Bake for 45-60 minutes at 180 °C (350 °F) or until cooked through.

Variations
Garlic bread: Melt 60 ml butter and add 6 crushed garlic cloves. Pour over bread dough and bake as directed.
Herb bread: Mix 40 ml chopped fresh herbs into the dough mixture. Bake as directed.
Onion bread: Mix 2 sautéed, finely chopped onions into the bread mixture. Bake as directed.

MISCELLANEOUS

Chutney cream dip

(48 servings; use ¼ or ½ of the quantities for 12 or 24 servings)

3 x 250 ml cream
6 garlic cloves, crushed
100-150 ml fruit chutney
30 ml lemon juice

Method
Mix all the ingredients and chill for 1 hour. Serve with crudités (see p. 81).

Cottage cheese dip

(48 servings; use ¼ or ½ of the quantities for 12 or 24 servings)

750 g chunky cottage cheese
100 ml chopped fresh parsley (or dill and oregano)
1 small onion, grated
salt and freshly ground black pepper to taste

Method
Mix all the ingredients and chill. Serve with crudités (see p. 81).

French dressing

(12 servings; use 2 or 4 times the quantities for 24 or 48 servings)

250 ml salad or olive oil
125 ml wine vinegar (or half vinegar and half lemon juice)
2 garlic cloves, crushed
5 ml French mustard
salt and black pepper to taste
10 ml salt

Method
Mix all the ingredients thoroughly and allow to stand for 2-3 hours for the flavours to develop.

Variations
Add 30 ml mayonnaise and 2 ml cayenne pepper to the basic recipe.
Greek dressing: Add 20 ml chopped fresh herbs and 1 finely chopped red chilli.

Croutons

(12 servings; use 2 or 4 times the quantities for 24 or 48 servings)

6 slices white bread, crusts removed, cut into 10 mm cubes
60 ml butter or cooking oil

Method
Fry the bread cubes in heated butter until golden brown and crisp.

Tip
☐ Add chopped fresh parsley or crushed garlic to the butter.

Caramel sauce

(12 servings; use 2 or 4 times the quantities for 24 or 48 servings)

2 large Bar-One chocolate bars
500 ml cream
5 ml vanilla essence

Method
Chop the Bar-Ones and melt them over low heat. Add the cream and vanilla essence and serve with ice cream.

DESSERTS

Pancake nests with fresh fruit

(12 servings; use 2 or 4 times the quantities for 24 or 48 servings)

12 small pancakes, 200 mm in diameter (see Crêpes suzettes recipe on p. 74)
250 ml custard
fresh strawberries and kiwi fruit
icing sugar for garnishing

Method
Press the pancakes into greased muffin pans to make nests. Bake for 10-15 minutes at 160 °C (325 °F) or until crisp. Turn out and allow to cool. Pour a little custard into the base of each nest and arrange the fresh fruit on top. Garnish with icing sugar. Serve immediately.

Tip
☐ Sprinkle the icing sugar through a tea strainer onto the dessert.

Crème caramel

(12 servings; make in separate 12-portion quantities for 24 or 48 servings)

Caramel Syrup
250 ml sugar
60 ml boiling water

Custard Mixture
30 ml sugar
4 eggs
2 egg yolks
1 ml salt
500 ml milk
5 ml vanilla essence

Method
Prepare the caramel syrup: Heat sugar in a saucepan over low heat until melted and golden in colour. Remove from the stove and add the boiling water. Stir over low heat until the caramel has dissolved. Pour the syrup into individual ovenproof dishes to cover the base.

Prepare the custard mixture: Beat the sugar, eggs, egg yolks, salt, milk and vanilla essence together and pour the mixture carefully on top of the caramel in the dishes. Place the dishes in a pan of hot water and bake for 45-60 minutes at 160 °C (325 °F) or until the custard mixture has set. Allow to cool and unmould.

Cinnamon dumplings

(12 servings; use 2 or 4 times the quantities for 24 or 48 servings, and cook 12 servings at a time)

500 ml (240 g) cake flour
20 ml baking powder
60 ml sugar
2 ml salt
60 ml butter
120 ml milk
1 egg
750 ml boiling water
125 ml sugar
15 ml ground cinnamon
30 ml butter

Method
Sift the dry ingredients together and rub in the butter. Beat the milk and egg and add to the dry ingredients. Mix well. Heat the water to boiling point in a saucepan and drop spoonfuls of dough into it. Cover and steam for 10-15 minutes without lifting the lid. Spoon out the dumplings into an ovenproof dish. Add sugar, cinnamon and butter to remaining sauce and heat to boiling point. Pour sauce over dumplings and serve immediately.

Variation
Caramel dumplings: Add 200 ml chopped glacé cherries and 100 ml chopped nuts to the batter. Before heating the water in the saucepan, caramelise 250 ml sugar in the pan. Add the boiling water and stir until the caramel dissolves. Follow the recipe given previously, omitting the cinnamon.

Vinegar pudding

(6 large servings; use 2, 4 or 8 times the quantities for 12, 24 or 48 servings and make in separate containers)

Batter
25 ml butter
125 ml sugar
2 eggs, beaten
25 ml apricot jam
375 ml (180 g) cake flour
10 ml ground ginger
1 ml cinnamon
1 ml salt
10 ml milk
5 ml bicarbonate of soda

Vinegar Syrup
500 ml water
500 ml sugar
125 ml vinegar

Method
First prepare the vinegar syrup: Cook the ingredients for 5-10 minutes over low heat. Allow to cool. Pour into an ovenproof dish.

Prepare the batter Cream the butter and sugar. Add the eggs and jam and mix thoroughly. Sift the dry ingredients, except the bicarbonate of soda, and add. Mix the milk and the bicarbonate of soda and add. Mix well. Drop spoonfuls of batter into the vinegar syrup and bake for 30-40 minutes at 180 °C (350 °F) or until golden brown.

Baked lemon pudding

(12 servings; use 2 or 4 times the quantities for 24 or 48 servings and make in separate containers)

350 ml sugar
75 ml butter
4 eggs, separated
juice and grated peel of 2 lemons
400-450 ml milk
50 ml cake flour

Method
Cream the sugar and butter. Add the egg yolks and beat well. Add the lemon juice and peel, milk and flour and mix to a smooth batter. Whisk the egg whites until soft peaks form and fold into the batter, using a metal spoon. Pour the batter into an ovenproof dish standing in a pan of boiling water and bake for 45 minutes at 180 °C (350 °F) or until set.

Mock cheesecake with gooseberries

(12 small servings; use 2 or 4 times the quantities for 24 or 48 servings, and make in separate containers)

125 ml lemon juice
10 g gelatine
1 can (397 g) condensed milk
5 ml grated lemon peel
1 tub (250 g) cream cheese

Crust
1 packet (200 g) Tennis biscuits, crumbled
100-125 ml melted butter

Fruit Topping
1 can (410 g) gooseberries
30 ml cornflour

Method
Heat a little of the lemon juice in a double boiler. Dissolve the gelatine in it. Allow to cool slightly, then add the condensed milk, remaining lemon juice and peel, stirring constantly. Cool for 20 minutes, then stir the cream cheese into the condensed milk mixture.

Prepare the crumb crust by mixing the biscuit crumbs thoroughly with the melted butter. Press into a pie dish 300 mm in diameter. Pour the condensed milk mixture into the crust and chill for 3-4 hours or until set.

Prepare the topping: Heat the drained gooseberry syrup and thicken it with cornflour mixed to a paste with water. Cool slightly. Arrange the gooseberries on top of the set condensed milk mixture and pour the thickened syrup evenly over them. Chill and serve with whipped cream.

Chocolate mousse

(6 very large servings; use 2, 4 or 8 times the quantities for 12, 24 or 48 large servings and make in separate containers)

250 g dark or white chocolate
5 eggs, separated
5 ml vanilla essence or Cointreau
5 ml coffee powder, dissolved in a little water
20 ml coffee liqueur
250 ml cream
10 ml grated orange peel

Method
Melt the chocolate in a double boiler and allow to cool slightly. Beat the egg yolks and add the chocolate gradually. Add the vanilla essence or Cointreau, coffee and liqueur. Whip the cream until stiff and fold into the chocolate mixture. Whisk the egg whites until soft peaks form and fold into the chocolate mixture. Chill for 2-3 hours. Garnish with grated orange peel.

Brandied peaches

(12 servings; use 2 or 4 times the quantity of peaches and 1½ or 3 times the quantity of sauce ingredients for 24 or 48 servings)

12 nectarines, halved and stoned

Brandy Sauce
500 ml water
250 ml sugar
2 cinnamon sticks
peel of 1 orange
4 whole cloves
15 ml lemon juice
50 ml brandy

Method
Prepare the brandy sauce: Boil the water, sugar, cinnamon, peel and cloves to a thin syrup (reduced to 250 ml). Drain the liquid and add the lemon juice and brandy. Blanch the peaches, drain them and pour the brandy sauce over. Refrigerate overnight.

Yoghurt with bananas

(12 servings; use 2 or 4 times the quantities for 24 or 48 servings)

1,5 litres natural full-cream yoghurt
6 bananas, sliced
240 g toasted nuts
120 ml honey

Method
Place the yoghurt in glass bowls. Arrange banana slices and nuts on top. Pour honey over.

Index